THE **POWER** OF CHOICES

7 steps to smarter decisions about work, life and success

JANINE WOODCOCK

The Power of Choices

ISBN 978-1-912300-25-9
eISBN 978-1-912300-26-6

Published in 2019 by SRA Books

The rights of Janine Woodcock to be identified as the author of this work has been asserted by her in accordance with the Copyright, Designs and Patents Act 1988.

A CIP record of this book is available from the British Library.

Illustrations by Tim Sutcliffe: www.timsutcliffe.co.uk

Printed in the UK.

'The right balance of challenge and support…
it's like being guided by a wise friend who's
committed to your development.'

Amanda Wylie

Head of Transformation, School of Management, University of Bath,
Co-founder, Reframe Your Future

'A raft of simple techniques to take back
control and get more from life.'

Alan Thorpe

Managing Director, Bray Leino CX

'Structured support to improve and sustain
your whole performance.'

Anita Fox

Head of Automotive, Facebook

'Understand how you connect to the world
around you so you can engage with it, manage
it and navigate through it.'

Lee Probert

College Chief Executive and Principal, York College

'Discover compelling reasons and strategies to
live your whole life differently.'

Mark Rogers

Executive Director, St James's Place Wealth Management

'A roadmap that's paid immediate dividends
across my work and home life.'

Derek Craig

Head of Marketing and Brand Communications,
Australian Institute of Company Directors

CONTENTS

Exercise worksheets are available to download from www.thepowerofchoices.net

PROLOGUE

The motorbike roars beneath us. My leather-clad body leans forward, holding on tight. My husband guides the bike through the twists and turns of the mountain roads, judging gaps, snaking through the traffic. A stretch of straight flat road; clutch clicks, gear drops, throttle opens. I feel the acceleration pull me backwards as Simon manoeuvres to overtake three cars. I hold on tighter. At 70 mph we are now alongside the second car we are overtaking, but he's judged it wrong and we are suddenly head on with a van. The driver in the car we are alongside looks at us in horror. A deafening noise as brakes screech. The van and our motorbike come to a stop no more than a centimetre away from each other. We get off the bike; the van driver gets out. Shouting, anger, more shouting. I am silent. In shock. Not in shock at what has just happened. In shock at what went through my mind as I anticipated the impact: 'It would be easier if I were dead – this could be a good thing…'

That moment was one in a series of catalysts that indicated something needed to change in my life. Outwardly, I portrayed a strong, driven, capable woman. Inwardly, I had lost my energy, optimism and resilience in a marriage with a man whose bipolar disorder was affecting every moment of our lives. I was lost in a cycle of putting everyone else's needs before mine. Lost in fear for my husband's life. (For 10 years of our 14-year marriage he was suicidal for at least six months a year.) Lost in my demanding career in marketing, which I loved but was using as a distraction from my traumatic home life. Lost in a cycle of using exercise as a way of escape to the point of it not being healthy. Lost in concerns for my family as my father was living with, and being treated for, prostate cancer.

Following on from that moment on the motorbike in 2008, something profound and fundamental in me shifted. For the first time in many years, I realised I had choices about things that I had previously felt obliged to do. Obligations that my mind had convinced me I wanted to fulfil. I finally gave myself the permission to take action. I made choices that were right for my own wellbeing and survival. Some of those choices were desperately difficult, and in making them I had to accept any consequences that were outside of my control and responsibility.

Now, many years later, I'd like to offer you a framework for making choices that drive and nourish your success in a way that is sustainable for you personally. My personal experiences coupled with my training and expertise as a leadership and executive coach combine to bring you the approach in this book.

IS THIS BOOK FOR YOU?

I am writing with you in mind if you think of yourself as driven, or if other people describe you as driven. This observation from others is important. If you are driven, you may not recognise the strength of your drive. For you, it's just a normal way of being. It's often other voices in your life that can give you perspective on how you actually are.

The relationship between drive and success is an interesting one and has itself been the subject of many books. In my work, I notice that driven people don't take much time to think about whether or not they are successful. They are always looking for the next thing they can do to become even more successful. They rarely stop and acknowledge themselves for something well done and often find it difficult to remember to offer that acknowledgement to others.

What's the relationship between your drive and your success? You may not even know what success means for you; it may be a loosely held thing, something akin to proving yourself. You may see yourself as strong and resilient, with an ability to overcome obstacles; to push yourself and keep going. You may have high standards and find you don't dwell on what hasn't worked as your focus is on what to do next. Whatever skills and behaviours you have that are linked to your drive, you are likely to value them deeply. They have served you well in your life up to this point.

When you hear people talking about trying to find a work-life balance, what do you think? Do you hear that as something other people need to do? Finding a work-life balance suggests an equality. If you are driven to succeed, you may not *want* to find a balance between work and life. You may feel work *is* life.

You are likely to be energised by, and enjoy, the challenge that your work brings.

My intention in this book is to give you a set of tools and techniques to make adjustments so you can sustain your success over the long term. Crucially, this is about sustaining it in a way that isn't to the detriment of other aspects of your life that you consider important. The tools will help you to get to know yourself better, so you can make better choices; choices that will enrich and enhance your experience of work and life; choices that will enable you to channel your drive in a way that nourishes you, rather than depletes you.

THE EVOLUTION OF THIS PROGRAMME

I have always had an in-built drive to succeed and used to get very frustrated by people around me who didn't have that same drive. Whilst I was writing this book, my mother sold and moved out of the family home of 50 years. During the decluttering of a lifetime of family paraphernalia, she found and returned to my brothers and me, things from our childhoods that had been squirreled away. My siblings and I had no idea any of it still existed; I was presented with old letters to my family from my travels, get well, birthday and anniversary cards I'd given to my parents, newspaper cuttings celebrating long forgotten competition wins, drawings and many exercise books and school projects from primary school. The timing was interesting. I came face to face with evidence of my younger self.

I found the following two extracts on the next page: one from an old school project when I was just nine years old; the other from a school report when I was 10. They show how fully formed my driven style was at a very young age.

My mum is Swiss and represented her country figure skating in the 1964 Winter Olympics. I grew up being so proud of her and believed I had inherited the drive that got her to that level of competition. My school and university achievements weren't outstanding (I enjoyed a party too much), but once I started working, I was lucky enough to find something I was really passionate about. After four years on a Barclays Bank graduate entry programme, I applied for a management role as Product Manager for the UK Current Account. It was a grade higher than I was expected to get after completing the full five years on the graduate programme, but I felt I was ready – I had nothing to lose. I applied and was successful. At the age of 25

> ## What I hate most
>
> I absolutely loathe peanut butter and broad beans, 'ugh'. And I hate wet people, who talk all slow and funny. I also hate, well not hate, but don't like untidyness very much. My bedroom is usually quite tidy but after a few days it gets rather messy and I feel as if I have to clear it up, otherwise I can't sleep, and would get up in the middle of the night and tidy it up.

Written by my nine-year-old self. I remember using the word 'wet' to describe people. It meant they didn't have strong opinions or quick answers, and/or spoke quietly (i.e. they weren't like me).

> General Remarks: Janine has worked very hard this year with very pleasing results. She has set herself a high standard and has maintained this throughout the year. She is a cheerful and helpful member of the class. A very good year. Well done!

Written by my Year 5 teacher when I was 10 years old. Those high standards were my early drive!

I had huge responsibility and I loved it. I especially enjoyed the elements where we created better experiences for our customers.

I led my internal teams and external marketing and data agencies to pioneer a number of firsts: we created the first current account transfer service in the UK; we pioneered the simplification of the overdraft application process; and rede-signed the current account statement to be much more than just a list of transactions (a statement that still exists today and became the benchmark for most statements as we know them).

By the age of 27 I'd had enough. I felt life in a large corporate wasn't for me. I left and went travelling for a year. Looking back, I can see that part of what I was escaping from was the stress and pressure I felt in the role. Much of that pressure was self-inflicted, as I took on more and more and revelled in the buzz and challenge of the projects I was working on.

On my return, I chose to immerse myself in the world of marketing. This had been the part of my degree and my Barclays role that I enjoyed the most. I chose to work for marketing agencies. For the next 25 years I applied my drive in the world of digital, data and direct marketing. I loved the fast, frenetic pace. I loved my creative and energetic colleagues, the range of clients we worked with and the strategic challenge of getting to know their key business drivers. I was addicted to the rush of pitching for new business, the even bigger rush of winning, the highs of a successful campaign and a happy client. Inevitably, those highs were offset by the crushing disappointments of losing pitches or clients. There were also many challenges: internal Board struggles as we went through various models of ownership and the difficulty of delivering what we sold (much of what we offered was on the cutting edge of innovation).

Alongside that hectic but fulfilling working life, I was married for 14 years to a man with very severe mental health issues (diagnosed after many years as bipolar disorder combined with narcissistic personality disorder). During the course of our relationship, his illness manifested itself more and more, and what

I used to call his 'normal self' – the man I met and fell in love with – gradually disappeared.

My drive repeatedly led me to make choices that had the intention of furthering my success, but that in reality were depleting my resilience and capability. Those choices also had unintended consequences in other important areas of my life and ultimately led to something in me breaking.

So, I write from the experience of being that driven and successful person. A person who had to stop, but who reconnected and found a healthier relationship with my drive. This allowed me to find success in a new context, with a whole new awareness of what I need to nourish that success.

I decided to take a master's level diploma in executive coaching and leadership development, initially with the intention of using those skills to help my clients and our agency. However, in coaching I found a new purpose and something I was hugely drawn to. I left the marketing world and set up my own business as a leadership development coach and consultant. Over the years since launching my own business, I started to notice a common pattern in my work with leaders. I noticed that they would be making many choices that were ultimately combining to undermine their capability to succeed. For example, they were reporting:

- 'I have to read my emails over the weekend.'
- 'I have to stay late to finish x, y and z.'
- 'I have to be there for my team whenever they need me.'

When we explored where the push for 'I have to' was coming from, it mostly came back to that person's own value set (cunningly disguised in their minds as pressure from their business or employer). There was often an underlying belief that their drive and work ethic were the keys to their success, and that if they didn't continue to prioritise work over other things, their success would slip away. I used to have that belief too. Employers love driven people because we keep taking things on. We are strong, we are resilient, we can overcome obstacles and we can push ourselves and keep going. However, we are often not great at knowing when to say no, or to step off the accelerator – just a little bit.

In my coaching work, a big part of what I do is to help my clients explore what choices they really have. From a feeling of being stuck and having a belief that there are no other choices, things suddenly start to open up. I see the difference in how my clients' drive shifts to focus on helpful strategies and conversations, rather than complaint about what is wrong and not working. Those shifts contribute to greater success because people can see the choices open to them for the first time. Crucially, the success is defined by them. The new choices are never to the detriment of their work but always of great benefit to them as a whole person, which in turn enhances their capability to succeed. This is very different to the burnout that so many driven people unfortunately experience (myself among them).

Making good choices comes from a place of strength and feeling that we have the ability to change something – it's a liberating word. 'Choices' is the word around which I have built the programme in this book.

Catalysts

Identify where your success is coming at the expense of other areas in your life that are important to you

Helpers & hinderers

Explore the strategies you use to support you through challenge to identify whether they are helpful, or if some of them unintentionally hinder you

Openness

Develop your skill in being open so you can hear challenge, support, criticism and encouragement

Insight

Identify the key beliefs and values that you need to shift in order to nourish and enable your future success

Care

Learn how to use your energy, optimise your resilience and move yourself forward when you feel stuck

Emergence

Connect with the new knowledge you have about yourself and identify how that will nourish your success

Sustain

Tools and techniques to sustain the choices you have decided to make during this programme

The Choices™ programme: overview

HOW TO USE THIS BOOK

This book will take you on a journey, and it may take you some time. Readers have described the experience of working through the programme as emotional, organic, creative and challenging. One reader observed that he felt it was a bit like seeing himself as a piece of pottery or ceramic – moulding, shaping, developing, improving.

You will work through each of the seven stages outlined above. Within each stage I'll offer you scientific theories, reference points and guidance to consider. I'll share examples from my own experience and those of my clients. (For privacy reasons names have been changed.)

Each stage of the programme has exercises for you to complete. Exercise worksheets are available to download from www.thepowerofchoices.net. (You'll see the download symbol where appropriate.) I suggest you download and print all the exercises, so you have them to hand as you work through the book.

I recommend that you start a notebook to have alongside you as you read. As you work through the book I'll encourage you to take notes, as well as complete the various exercises using the downloadable worksheets. Your additional notes are as important as the exercises. They will be useful for you to refer back to as you move towards the end of the programme and pull all your thinking together. This is not a quick-fix self-help book. It's an exploration for you to take at your own pace.

Working through the programme may be an experience different to any you've had before. Here are a few pointers to help you fully engage with what follows:

- Create time to work through each stage. Choose a space that feels creative and inspiring where you can focus and be uninterrupted.
- The exercises often need space away from the book for you to think. Give yourself that space and complete the exercises when you are ready.
- Trust the process and resist the temptation to focus on an endgame.
- Don't rush the programme.
- Let your subconscious do its thing. Allow your brain space to reflect, often.
- Take breaks between exercises and chapters.

ADDITIONAL SUPPORT

Some of this work may bring up challenges that you feel you need extra support to work through or they may surface unexpected and unusual emotions that you need help in processing. Towards the end of the book (on page 197) I offer guidance on how to select an executive coach or, indeed, a therapeutic practitioner (for example, a counsellor).

The time you choose to invest in yourself and your future success by reading this book will be time well spent. I hope you enjoy the process as it unfolds and that you are left with a new relationship with your drive and how it can nourish your success.

CHAPTER 1

INTRODUCTION

This chapter starts the process of helping you identify where you may be succeeding in work at the expense of other areas in your life that are important to you. It will help you tune into the apparently little things that you may be ignoring – things that you feel are simply irritating, inconvenient and getting in the way of your success. I call these little things 'catalysts'.

You've probably already had moments in your life where an experience has crystallised your thinking and helped you (or forced you) to change your status quo. For example, people often talk about the epiphany of surviving a life-threatening event and how that reshapes their mindset. In our work together, I am not looking at the extreme experience of a life-threatening event, I'm looking at more everyday things. Things that you may see as mundane but that could actually be significant. Our attention is always grabbed by the big catalyst. In my coaching work, clients will often describe one massive catalyst that forces them to take stock and adjust. But further discussions reveal a myriad of smaller catalysts that had built up to that point – together with the realisation that they'd been ignored.

For example, take Jill – a successful business consultant in the pharmacology field. At the peak of her career, Jill was enjoying a busy and fulfilling work and private life.

One night, Jill was working late (again) and waiting for some crucial test results for a client project to come through from overseas. She had let the rest of her team go home because she was concerned about their wellbeing. Jill was absolutely exhausted and, while she knew she needed to rest, she felt she had no choice but to push on. This was not the first time Jill had worked this late. She described to me something going 'pop' in her body. A hot, red, raised rash appeared all over her. Despite this very unusual and unsettling experience, Jill didn't feel she could stop working, so ploughed on.

Although there is no dramatic end to this story (the rash went away the next day and she suffered no other ill effects), the moment was the catalyst for Jill to start the process of looking at what choices she was making in her life. The physiological response to her stress, anxiety and exhaustion was so unusual, visual and concerning that Jill was forced to accept she was operating on overdrive and needed to take her foot off the gas, for a short while, to re-energise and restore.

The thing about the big catalyst that stops you is that it's never ever the first one. The showstopper catalyst never ever comes out of the blue. You'll have experienced many mini-catalysts and allowed them to bubble away, often for months or years. All those little things will have seemed trivial, annoying and insignificant, so you ignore them. They then become normalised over time and you just see them as part of who you are. Once they've become normalised and are part of you, they're very hard to recognise as being problematic. In fact, we often start to see these things as a contributor to our drive and success. We fail to notice these smaller valuable clues until a big catalyst comes and stops us in our tracks.

This chapter will help you identify these catalysts. It will help you make new connections between your choices and these catalysts and start to shape where you may want to make positive changes.

Persevere with any discomfort in these exercises and perhaps the feeling of being a little out of control and not knowing what's going to come up next. Trust me; the benefits will be worth it. Remember, the goal here is to sustain your success over time, rather than head for the potential of your body (or mind) making you stop.

THE MIND-BODY CONNECTION

There is more and more research and published academic work on the mind-body connection. One of the most compelling books I've read on the subject is by Gabor Maté M.D. In his 2019 revision of his 2003 book *When the Body Says No: The Cost of Hidden Stress*[1], Maté shares many case studies illustrating how the hidden cost of stress shows up in our bodies. He demonstrates how autoimmune diseases, inflammatory illnesses and certain hormonal-based cancers can all be triggered by living with high levels of stress (even if we feel that stress is good). I found the depth of the case studies, the consistency in the findings and the range of stress-related conditions very confronting. I identified with the underlying drive to succeed and many of his patients' life stories. Reading Maté's work reinforced my purpose behind this book; good choices are essential to nourish us.

Back pain is probably the most widely accepted symptom that can be attributed to overwork and/or stress (when there is no underlying medical issue such as a slipped disc). There is also growing evidence and acceptance of the mind-gut connection and how mental fatigue can create gut issues. There are many available resources on this to explore, but one of note is the TED article by Diego Bohórquez, a neuroscientist at Duke University[2]. His research into the gut-brain connection has revealed new connections that may change how we treat conditions as varied as anorexia, irritable bowel syndrome, autism and PTSD (post-traumatic stress disorder).

---

1   Maté, G. (2019) *When the Body Says No: The Cost of Hidden Stress*, 2nd Edition, Vermillion
2   https://ideas.ted.com/a-scientist-explores-the-mysteries-of-the-gut-brain-connection/

My experience, combined with reading many articles over the years, leads me to the following conclusion: if you are repeatedly experiencing physiological symptoms and general medical advice is unable to find a cause, the chances are you need to look to your mindset, beliefs and lifestyle to try and shift things.

My love for my work meant I chose to work long hours (typically 60–70 hours a week). I worked in a high adrenaline, fast-paced culture that I loved and felt alive in. The low-level back and neck problems I had experienced for many years started to get worse, but that was an easy one to explain away. I had had a nasty fall from a horse in my early twenties, which had resulted in severe whiplash. I blamed the NHS for not having treated it with physio at the time and blamed the fact that I was driving over 35,000 miles a year (a daily two-hour driving commute and travel to clients). I recognised that I was not doing enough exercise, but ironically didn't pay huge attention to that because I was too busy, prioritising the work I loved over everything else, alongside caring for my husband and his deteriorating mental health (which was fluctuating between long bouts of severe, debilitating depression and periods of mania or hypomania and narcissism). The neck and back problems increased. I got to the point where I couldn't drive for a period of two months because I was unable to turn my head to look over either shoulder. I had private healthcare through work and, despite years of MRI scans, physiotherapy and osteopathy, there was still no 'diagnosis'. The various specialists gently probed about the nature of my work and home life and asked whether I thought stress could be contributing to my pain. I wasn't ready to hear that there was anything other than an 'outside' problem that was causing the issues.

My internal narrative at that time was as follows: I am good with stress. It energises me. My agency needs me. My husband needs me. I have the skills and resilience to help everybody. My ability to cope with high levels of stress is part of being driven. I am really strong.

Due to my severe back problems, and because I felt my husband needed me to be nearer home more often, I eventually decided to change jobs. I found a fantastic role on the board of a local, independently-owned marketing agency. I swapped the two-hour daily drive to and from work for a 90-minute walk. Over eight months I lost two stone and my neck/back problems started to improve. My passion for this new company and its potential gave me renewed energy and a sense of purpose outside of my home life. The time I got back from not commuting was now invested in my new team and my clients. I was still supporting my husband financially and emotionally – the support calls and texts continued – but he was now able to meet me after work or for lunch.

My back had improved, but I started to experience a number of other low-level health niggles: recurrent colds, cold-sores, headaches, dizziness – all of these would come and go fairly regularly. They were never enough to stop me or make me pay attention to what they may be symptomatic of. They were an irritation to what I wanted to achieve. I could see there was a link between working hard and some of these things (the classic holiday cold), but I expected myself to be stronger, and was annoyed that my body was 'letting me down'. The health niggles didn't fit with my ongoing self-identification of being strong and resilient.

You will have developed a way of 'being' in your career; a leadership or management style that, to this point, has been useful in getting you to where you are now. There are already some great books available on specific leadership styles and how you may need to adapt these over time (see, for example, Marshall Goldsmith's 2008 *What Got You Here Won't Get You There*). However, the focus of this chapter is not to look at your broader leadership style, but to identify whether you are displaying any behaviours that could suggest you are operating at the edge of your capacity. As a driven person, there is often the temptation to think your capacity is infinite, and that you 'should' be able to cope with increasing demands across all areas of your life. You may have a superb level of resilience and capability, but we are all human, and therefore all have limits. If you are scoffing at that statement, there is even more reason to read on.

Physiological catalyst identifier

This will help you tune into your physiology.

You may find this difficult, especially when your focus as a driven person is likely to be very outward and goal orientated. You are likely to be focused on finding answers quickly and deciding on concrete actions so you can move forward. In pursuit of that, you may have developed a great skill of ignoring (or justifying) things that are not conducive to your long-term success. You may even think you've fixed something, and then not pay attention to what follows.

This exercise has three parts: a body map; looking at levels of discomfort; and focusing on what you now know.

PART 1: BODY MAP

Take five deep slow breaths, in through the nose, out through the mouth. Focus your breath in your stomach and diaphragm. If you are feeling your breath is shallow and up in your chest, take as long as you need to focus on getting your breathing into your belly.

On the last outbreath close your eyes and mentally scan down your body from the crown of your head to your toes. Take five minutes to sit and check in with every sensation you feel.

Now you are 'in your body' look at the diagram and, either in your notebook or on your downloadable work-sheet, mark where on your body you are experiencing any symptoms of discomfort at the moment (use numbers for each area of discomfort).

Next, add in any additional areas of discomfort that you regularly experience, no matter how small.

Then, for each numbered area of discomfort make some notes about the nature of the discomfort. This will help you remember what you were thinking about when you look back at this exercise.

After you've made your notes, I recommend that you ask a few of the people who know you well to see if there's anything additional that they notice you suffering with. This is important. Don't underestimate how your drive can make it hard for you to notice things, even when you're trying your hardest to tune in!

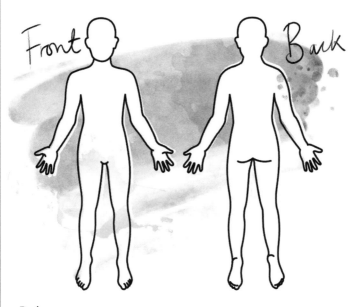

Body map

PART 2: DISCOMFORT LEVELS

Use the worksheet grid to plot each numbered area from Part 1 according to level of discomfort and frequency. For example, using my experience outlined above, I would write 'back pain' in the top right-hand corner of the grid.

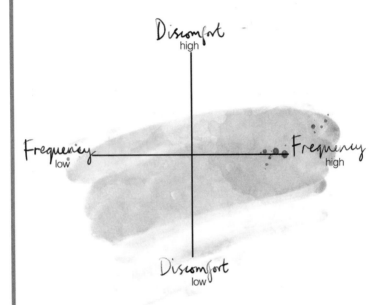

Discomfort and frequency grid

PART 3: WHAT DO YOU NOW KNOW?

Now ask yourself the following questions, making notes in your notebook or on your worksheet.

- Which symptoms am I ignoring?
- Which symptoms am I paying attention to?
- Do any of these symptoms seem to occur around certain situations/events, or when I am feeling a certain way?
- Which symptoms have the most negative impact (day-to-day and/or over the longer term)?

EXERCISE REVIEW

- How do you feel having completed this exercise?
- Did it trigger any particular emotions such as irritation or impatience?
- Did you find it hard to identify some of the catalysts yourself?
- What do you take away from this, and what will you do differently as a result?

Psychological catalyst identifier

This exercise will help you with self-awareness of your mood and demeanour.

When completing the table on the worksheet try to be objective and open. When driven people complete this there can be a tendency to justify certain behaviour and therefore not really notice it.

> *John was aware that he used to snap at people. Yet, when he spoke about his awareness he would explain that he only resorted to snappiness when he had to tell someone something for the third time. So, while he was aware, he saw the reason for his snappiness as the other person's inability to retain information. His justification for his behaviour meant his awareness was fleeting, and therefore not something he fully noticed.*

Below, tick the box that corresponds with your level of agreement with each statement.

   1 = Strongly agree

   2 = Agree

   3 = Neutral

   4 = Disagree

   5 = Strongly disagree

To help you build your awareness, ask some people for their view of the above: how do they see you?

	1	2	3	4	5
I laugh a lot during my day					
I don't get easily irritated					
I am able to switch off from work easily					
I am very happy to be challenged					
I am rarely defensive					
I don't often snap at people					
I am patient with people					
I have energy to spend time with my family					
I have energy to spend time with my friends					
I feel energised when I get up					
I feel optimistic about the future					
I feel stimulated by my life					
I rarely lose my temper					
I feel I can be myself at work					

EXERCISE REVIEW

If you have a high number of ticks in disagree or strongly disagree, your general mood is suggesting some underlying issue that you may not be addressing.

Now take some time to:

- Look at those statements you've marked as neutral and force yourself to make a choice of either agree or disagree.

- Looking at the things you have marked as disagree or strongly disagree, ask yourself the following (making notes as you go):

  - What things might be triggering these behaviours in me?

  - How do other people experience me when I display these behaviours?

  - Which of these behaviours do I want to shift away from?

RELATIONSHIPS AS CATALYSTS

For many years, friends would say things like, 'You're working too hard, give yourself a break' or 'We never see you any more'. They'd show concern when I was really exhausted. I used to listen, but didn't really hear them. I'd just think they didn't understand me – their complaints usually hit on behaviours that I believed contributed to my success. I've always wanted to be successful. I worked at Board level from 1998, enjoyed my work and always wanted to do the best I could for my company and my clients. My drive was such that work and my clients were my priority. Because of this, I rarely accepted invites from friends to see them on weekday evenings; if I was needed at work, I'd put that first. I never committed to any evening classes that might have nurtured me creatively. I had various gym member- ships, but I didn't make much use of them. I did, however, allow myself to accept Friday evening and weekend invites (whoo hoo!). But on a Friday, I very often showed up late to com- mitments. One event that really sticks in my mind was when I turned up for a dinner party at 8 pm (half an hour late). My husband was already there. The hosts and other guests looked shocked when I actually turned up. They didn't ask about my week, they just carried on chatting. I felt weirdly disconnected from them. It was a shock when I realised that I wasn't enjoying the company of my closest friends and was thinking I might as well have stayed at work; another of my catalysts for change.

Often in my coaching conversations, clients will repeat things that are said to them by loved ones. They'll report the conversation in an almost jovial 'isn't this amusing' way...

Here's an example:

Peter: *I love my job, it's crazy and busy, and I have to be available all the time. I love the buzz. As I work globally, I'm literally available 24/7 365. My son joked to me the other day that I love my laptop and phone more than him [laughter].*

Me: *Your son feels that you love your laptop and phone more than him?*

Peter: *Yes, but he doesn't understand that I have to be available all the time.*

Me: *Do you love your laptop and phone more than your son?*

Peter: *No – of course not.*

Me: *Is it important to you that your son knows you don't love your laptop and phone more than you love him?*

Peter: *Yes, really important but my work's important, too. It's 24/7. That's just the way it is.*

Me: *So, it's really important that your son knows you love him more than your laptop and phone, but 24/7 is just the way it is?*

Peter: *Well, yes.*

Me: *So, if 24/7 is the way it is, but you want your son to know you love him more than your laptop, what needs to happen next?*

...and from that point in the conversation the client could suddenly access some simple choices he could make to shift things (for example, not having his phone on at mealtimes). The starting point is often that we feel there are no options to change things. Things are just the way they are. But we always have choices.

Relationship catalyst identifier

This exercise will help you tune in differently to what you may be hearing from people who care for you.
It isn't intended to help you if any of your important relationships are in difficulty due to a more systemic incompatibility or other relationship breakdown.

Take some time to think about things you are hearing from the following groups of people. Think about comments or statements of concern linked to your work/moods/time spent with them. If nothing comes to mind, ask them what their regular worries or concerns about you are (in relation to your work). Make notes in your notebook.

1   Things that my partner (or person you have the closest relationship with) tends to say to me.
2   Things my family might say to me.
3   Things my friends are saying to me.
4   Things my work colleagues and/or clients are saying to me.

EXERCISE REVIEW
Looking back at the above, ask yourself:

- Are there any consistent themes in what people are saying?
- How do I respond to them when they offer these comments?
- What do I think their motivation is in offering me these comments?

5   In relation to each of the comments, where am I on the spectrum below?

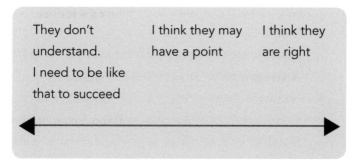

They don't
understand.
I need to be like
that to succeed

I think they may
have a point

I think they
are right

6   From the comments I am now connecting with, is there anything specific that I need to pay attention to as being a potential catalyst?

Wheel of focus

This exercise will help you look at where you are expending your energy. It will help you to check in on whether that feels right for you, in the context of how you manage your drive for success alongside other important aspects of your life.

With this exercise you are working with categories in a wheel that represent all the areas in your life. I've suggested categories on the worksheet, but you can use your own if that feels more meaningful. I've listed the categories below in alphabetical order to avoid any inference of importance, with clarification notes where I felt they were needed:

● Exercise
● Family

- Finances – energy and focus on financial wellbeing of your personal life (not your business life – this would be included in the 'work' element on the chart)
- Friends
- Interests/hobbies – this excludes exercise, which is listed separately
- Nutrition
- Physical environment – this is about the time you spend thinking about/being aware of where you are when you work rest and play
- Romantic relationship
- Sleep
- Social media – this relates to personal use of social media (i.e. not posting or managing social media for your business – that would fall under 'work')
- Wellbeing/relaxation
- Work

The exercise has three parts:

1   Where are you now?
2   Where do you want to be?
3   Which categories require the biggest shift?

PART 1: WHERE ARE YOU NOW?

Using the worksheet, choose one coloured pen to mark how much focus/energy you are currently giving to each category? By focus/energy, I mean your level of satisfaction with the time you spend (mind-time or action/doing-time) in each category.

  0 = Totally unsatisfied
10 = Totally satisfied

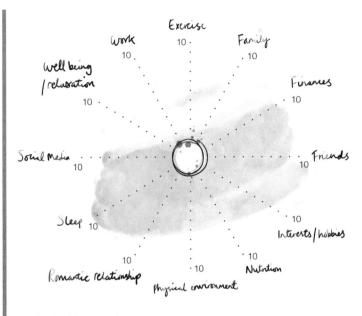

Wheel of focus

PART 2: WHERE DO YOU WANT TO BE?

Using a different coloured pen, mark how much focus/
energy you would like to give to each category?

As you consider this, try and put aside any inner voice
that starts to tell you what may or may not be possible.
For example, you may be thinking you'd love to give more
energy to a hobby, but you haven't got time. Put your effort
into considering this question from the perspective that
anything is possible. And be honest with yourself. There is
no judgement here – what you feel/want is yours. If you're
not spending much focus/energy on your family, there is no
judgement that you should. This is about you reconnecting
with what you want to do. You may have lost sight of this in
the face of your drive.

PART 3: WHICH CATEGORIES REQUIRE THE BIGGEST SHIFT?

Looking at your wheel, circle those categories where there is the biggest gap between where you are now and where you'd like to be.

List the circled categories in order of the shift you want to see; start with those requiring the biggest shift at the top of your list.

EXERCISE REVIEW

What emotions arose for you as you completed this exercise? Pay attention to:

- negative thoughts
- positive thoughts
- emotions (anger, sadness, guilt, frustration, elation, joy).

If you can, capture what it was in the exercise that triggered those emotions.

This exercise may be bringing up some things that surprise you, or it may be reinforcing things you already knew instinctively. You may have categories where you want to make significant shifts, or there may not be much shift needed at all.

Either way, you now have an idea of where to focus your attention and energy in looking at how to nourish your success.

REFLECTION

This chapter has given you a number of ways to identify catalysts that are pointing towards the fact that you may not be nourishing your success in a way that's sustainable for you.

Make a note here or in your notebook of the areas that you have identified in each exercise that you want to focus on.

Physiological catalysts to pay attention to:

Psychological catalysts to pay attention to:

Relationship catalysts to pay attention to:

Areas of focus – where to make some changes:

As you work through this book, keep coming back to this chapter. Add in new catalysts that you become aware of. In later chapters, we look at how to approach dealing with those catalysts that are important for you, and how to create the shifts you want to see.

From this point forward, when you next experience any of the catalysts you've identified, reflect and make notes (mental or written) as follows:

- What happened before the catalyst (minutes, hours and/ or days)?
- When did you notice that the catalyst had gone?
- When you noticed it was gone, did focusing back in on it make it reappear?

This reflective approach is part of the discipline required to build and enhance your self-awareness, which in turn will enable you to step into understanding how to create an evolved version of you that can sustain your success over the long term.

CHAPTER 2

Helpers & hinderers

INTRODUCTION

To get where you are in your career to date, you'll have developed a range of coping strategies to respond to all the challenges that have come your way. This chapter helps you look at these strategies to assess whether or not they are indeed helping you. Some choices may feel good in the moment but may have unintended longer-term effects – effects that could actually hinder your success; the very opposite to your intended outcome. Even as you read that last sentence you may already be aware of some of those potential hinderers. Your inner voice might be talking up quite loudly right now, commenting on what you 'should' and 'shouldn't' be doing. I'm not a fan of shoulds and shouldn'ts. These always come from an outside voice of judgement. My intention in this chapter is to give you the tools, reference points and exercises to help you make the choices that are right for you. Choices that will help you nourish your success. You'll be able to consider your current choices in the context of the catalysts you identified in Chapter 1 and decide what you want to change and adapt moving forward.

YOUR RELATIONSHIP WITH STRESS

A driven mindset can see stress as an integral and necessary part of success. I know my own drive used to crave that buzz, which I used to call good stress. While I was aware of this good stress and how it energised me, I couldn't engage with the concept of bad stress. My belief was that any stress was good and that I had the strength, drive and determination to harness what I needed from it. As you've seen in Chapter 1, I ignored the physiological elements of stress and had no awareness that cumulative high-stress situations were eroding my resilience over time.

In this chapter you'll see that the buzz has the potential to tip into something that damages your success. One of the keys to making choices that nourish your success is being able to develop a strong awareness of your stress triggers, as well as tuning into what type of stress you are experiencing.

To help people tune into their levels of stress, I find it useful to encourage people to:

- recognise that stress is both a psychological and physio-logical experience[3] (i.e. it impacts both our mind and our body)
- accept that everyone has their own unique response to stress, depending on life experiences and biological vul-nerability. Accepting this can help you move yourself away from denial and/or self-judgement of 'I should be able to cope with this'.

---

3 Schneiderman, N., Ironson, G. and Siegel, S. D. (2018) 'Stress and Health: Psychological, Behavioral, and Biological Determinants', *Annual Review of Clinical Psychology* 1 (2005): 607–628

- move away from a black and white view of stress, i.e. it's good or bad. It's more useful (and accurate) to recognise that we experience stress on a spectrum.

Looking at the types of stress along the spectrum I find the Yerkes–Dodson law a useful reference[4]. The Yerkes–Dodson law suggests that performance increases with physiological or mental arousal, but only up to a point. This can usefully be illustrated using a curve:

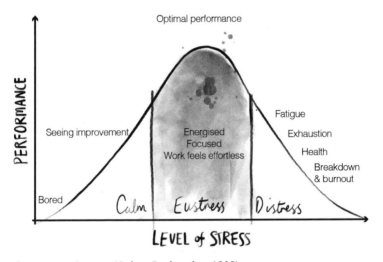

Stress curve (source: Yerkes–Dodson law 1908)

As a driven person, what do you need to take from this model?

- **Calm**: whilst this is an important zone to spend some time in for overall wellbeing, spending too long here will lead you to stagnate and get bored. The fact that you're reading this book, suggests that you will be very aware of when you are in this zone. You won't like it. It is too boring. You're

4 Teigen, K. H. (1994) 'Yerkes-Dodson: A Law for all Seasons', *Theory & Psychology*, 4(4), pp.525–547

probably already great at getting yourself out of here and into action on to the next exciting thing.

- **Eustress** (aka good stress): this is when we feel fully energised and motivated. Academics in the field of positive psychology have coined the term 'flow[5]', which relates to being in this zone. When we are in flow we are completely immersed, our brains are working to their optimum. Sometimes we are so focused that the rest of the world disappears from our awareness.
- **Distress** (aka bad stress): if you stay in the distress zone for extended periods of time, your fatigue can lead to exhaustion, exhaustion can lead to ill health, and ill health can lead to breakdown and burnout.

No one chooses to end up in the distress end of the curve, or wants to experience breakdown and burnout. Yet, so many successful people do. I did. Why? It is simply this. If you are driven and successful, your belief in how hard you *should* be working will fool your brain into ignoring your symptoms.

In Chapter 1, you've already identified the catalysts that could indicate you're in the distress zone. Continue to pay attention to those – they're your early warning system. But they will only help you move out of the distress zone if you heed their warnings and pay attention to all the things you are doing to try and offset that stress (your helpers or hinderers).

I used to regularly push myself to the point of being in the bad-stress zone, especially when I had a role that was purely focused on leading and winning new business pitches. It's a fine balance; the goal was to maintain optimal performance,

---

5 https://positivepsychologyprogram.com/mihaly-csikszentmihalyi-father-of-flow/

but the reality was that I was making choices that consistently pushed me into the distress zone. I would somehow summon the energy to work late, over weekends or whatever was required to get myself and the team in the best possible shape to win the pitch. These pitches sometimes extended over nine or 10 months, and a number of them would be running concurrently. I thought I was excellent at managing my energy levels. In the medium term, things weren't too bad, but over time my choices started to take their toll.

HOW STRESS AFFECTS THE BODY

I believe that if you can understand how your body works, you are more likely to be able to make choices that are appropriate to you. This is a huge field of science and study. My intention here is to bring you an accessible version of the various theories.

Stress can create the fight or flight response in our body. This is a physiological response from way back in our ancestry and can be vital (for example, to run away from something) and of benefit to help the immune system speed up its responses (for example, healing a wound). It's that feeling of adrenaline rush. You may be brilliant at, and even enjoy, the feeling of this level of stress for short amounts of time. And you may be using this as part of your strategy to succeed.

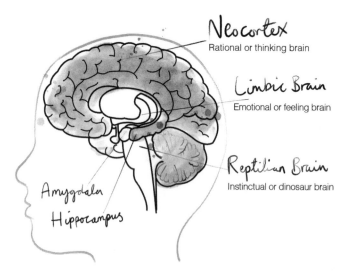

A simplified view of the primary areas of the brain associated with stress response

So what happens physiologically when we are in fight or flight?

- It is our amygdala (in our limbic brain) that fires our fight or flight response. The amygdala is a very primitive part of our brain, so we have no control over this response. It happens in a split second before you are aware what's happening.

- The response triggers a series of chemical messengers (including cortisol and adrenaline) that flood our body and activate our endocrine system.

- The endocrine system is the collection of glands that produce hormones that regulate metabolism, growth and development, tissue function, sexual function, reproduction, sleep, and mood, among other things. It affects almost every cell and organ in our body.

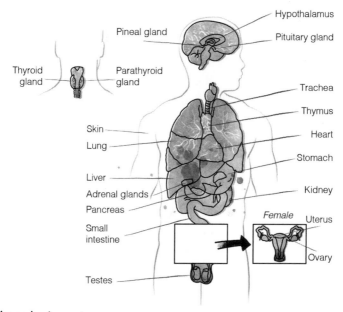

The endocrine system

● Based on the level of bad stress we are experiencing, our endocrine system makes choices on where to shut down and save energy to cope with the distress. The first to be shut down is the blood flow to your skin, digestive organs, kidneys, your immune systems and reproductive systems.

Your body is designed to only stay in fight or flight mode for a short amount of time. After the perceived threat has passed, your body's physiology expects to return to normal functioning within minutes. However, in your day-to-day life the definition of a perceived threat can be a myriad of things, and these things can happen one after the other – meaning you stay in fight or flight mode for a sustained period of time. Modern-day threats that can trigger fight or flight can be as simple as an irritating email from a colleague or missing a train connection on the way to a vital meeting. If you get easily triggered and stay in bad stress for sustained periods of time, you will have elevated levels of stress hormones coursing through your body. Your endocrine system will continue to prevent important hormones flowing, mostly affecting the kidney and liver (both of which play a key role in digestion) and heart. Over time, this imbalance will start to have a negative effect on your wellbeing.

Driven people tend not to remember much about the nature of challenges; they remember how they overcame them. Going back over past events may not be something you do very much. In fact, this in itself can be part of our survival strategy. While this is a hugely positive trait, ignoring the past could mean you are disengaged with the factors that may contribute to a current physiological experience. When I looked back over time to understand my stressors I forgot my mum's triple heart bypass surgery, which had happened at the same

Mark was Managing Director of an SME by the time he was 28. His wife worked as a nurse, and they had three children and a very large dog. Mark was a man with a strong work ethic and principles, who cared deeply about his business and team. The demands of his job as MD were significant, as was the pull from his home life. He suffered a number of low-level colds, but kept pushing on through and ignoring them. Members of the team were feeding back to him that they were concerned. Mark's wife was worried and also expressed her concern – with increasing frequency. He listened to, but took no notice of, all of the concern.

Mark came into the office one day with blue lips and pale skin, clearly not well at all. His PA forced him to go to the doctor where he was diagnosed with double pneumonia and sent straight to hospital. Double pneumonia aged 28 in an outwardly healthy young man.

Everyone was shocked, but he'd ignored all of his catalysts. The pressure of work and life had him operating in fight or flight mode and his endocrine system wasn't functioning. Ultimately, his body forced him to stop, after which he was off work for three months.

Mark returned with a different relationship to his drive and was able to make better choices in how he worked; choices that nourished his future success.

time that my dad was desperately ill with cancer and receiving radiotherapy. It never ceases to amaze me how our brains can delete information. We may delete it but, at a cellular level, our bodies remember it.

If you are interested in reading more around this, it is well referenced in *The Body Keeps the Score*[6]. In this book, physician, researcher and teacher Bessel van der Kolk M.D. explores how traumatic experiences impact our physical (and mental) health even decades after the event.

Stress identifiers

There are two exercises within this section.

1 STRESS PROPENSITY IDENTIFIER

This exercise will help you understand whether you are operating in an extended fight or flight state.

You may not believe you are operating in a fight or flight mode as your perception is you don't feel threatened. However, if you are driven to succeed, you could be creating the fight or flight response in your body simply by doing what you do naturally. You may enjoy the sensation of being busy and achieving all the time. Without you being aware of it, the primal instincts in your brain could be seeing everyday events as hazards that you need to 'fight' against, which may mean you are living with elevated levels of stress hormones (cortisol, adrenaline and norepinephrine) in your body.

---

6   Van der Kolk, B. A. (2014) *The Body Keeps the Score: Brain, Mind, and Body in the Healing of Trauma*, Penguin

Complete the following table or use the worksheet version.

1=Strongly agree

2=Agree

3=Neutral

4=Disagree

5=Strongly disagree

	1	2	3	4	5
I love working in a high-pressured, fast-paced environment. I love the buzz.					
I find I am most productive working towards an imminent deadline.					
I feel sluggish in the morning but wired and awake in the evening.					
I struggle to focus on important in-depth/complex tasks as my mind is racing on to the next thing.					
If I have down-time, I have to find something to do. I can't just sit around.					

If you noted agree or strongly agree to more than three of the above, you are likely to be operating in a fight or flight state more often or for longer than is good for you. The challenge here is that if you've been operating like this for a long time, it will feel normal. It can even be addictive, in the sense that you'll need more and more adrenaline and cortisol to get the same buzz. Therefore, you seek out more and more stimulants to get that buzz. As a consequence, you may feel mentally that you are in your good-stress zone, but physiologically you are in the bad-stress zone. (Remember, stress is a psychological and physiological experience.)

EXERCISE REVIEW

Now that you understand a bit more about how your body works, and the parts of your body that can be affected by bad stress, have a look back at the three types of catalysts you identified in Chapter 1:

- Physiological
- Psychological
- Relationship

For each of the above, consider the following questions and make notes:

- Is there a relationship between any of the catalysts I noted and what I now understand about how the body works?
- Which of my catalysts are being triggered by being in the bad-stress zone?

2 STRESS IDENTIFIER TIMELINE

This exercise will help you connect with the past and give you a perspective on how your stress has evolved over recent times. It will help you notice any behaviour patterns that may have emerged without you being consciously aware of them.

I've offered some different grid options in the online worksheet to help you capture your thinking. Alternatively, you can create your own. Using your choice of grid style, note down the key events of the last three years. If there are significant events in prior years, note those too. Have a chat with some people you are close to, to see if they remember anything you might have missed.

Choose a way of marking positive, neutral or negative events on your timeline. I use coloured circles (red/amber/green), but you could also use emoji-style faces. What is important here is that you connect with whatever you write.

As you do this, be aware that it can be quite draining to think back over past years and bring up memories of stresses that you may have forgotten about. Given this, please choose an appropriate time when you have the energy to tackle this exercise, and don't plan anything too demanding afterwards.

I completed my first stress timeline seven years ago, when my mind and my body conspired and forced me to stop and take time out. After finally agreeing with my doctor that I needed to stop, I took three months off work. It was hugely impactful to look at the timeline and accept the level of fight or flight I had been operating at for such a long period of time. Over a period of ten years I was operating in the belief that I was coping. I was finding life incredibly tough, but I was tough. Being strong and able to cope with whatever life threw at me was part of my identity. Seeing the timeline in black and white started to help me accept reality and started the process of understanding my catalysts and their triggers.

In the course of writing this book, I updated my stress timeline. I've included it below as an example. As it's black and white, you can't see the coloured circles I've created, but red (negative) experiences show as a darker grey. It's been interesting to revisit this, and energising to see how my choices have created significant shifts from red/amber to green since my major catalyst in 2008.

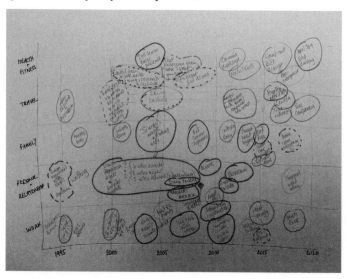

EXERCISE REVIEW

I suggest you take a break and then come back to your timeline and consider the following questions:

- What do you notice in this visual representation of your last three years?
- Note down any feelings that may have come up in response to this exercise.
- Looking back at the work you did on your catalysts in Chapter 1, is there any link between your times of bad stress and the catalysts you have identified?
- What do you now know?
- What will you do with that knowledge?

Stress-relief strategies

Everyone has their own way of dealing with stress. So far in this chapter, you've looked at where you are in terms of bad stress and good stress. The next two exercises will help you look at your stress helpers.

1 STRESS HELPERS

Using the grid on the worksheet (or an adapted version of your own), note down the things you turn to/strategies you use when you are in each of the three areas of stress. Be really honest here – write down everything you can think of.

It's normal and human to not be aware of, or remember, everything we do. I recommend you ask those closest to you what they notice you doing in response to stress. Be open to what they say. Don't fight their observations if you don't like them. (For example, the amount of alcohol people drink is often a contentious point.) Accept their observations and add them to the chart (in a different colour if you find it useful to distinguish).

Things I do when I feel...	Stress zone		
	Calm	Good stress (eustress)	Bad stress (distress)
Exercise			
Family			
Friends			
Interests/ hobbies			

Things I do when I feel...	Stress zone		
	Calm	Good stress (eustress)	Bad stress (distress)
Food and drink			
Sleep			
Social media			
Wellbeing/ relaxation			
Work			

EXERCISE REVIEW

Looking back at your stress helper grid, now consider the following:

- Are all your activities focused in one or a few categories (rows on the table)?
- Do you notice anything about your main 'go-to' activities when you are in the bad-stress mode?
- If this grid had been completed by one of your closest friends and they were sharing it with you, what advice might you give them?
- What do you think about your stress helpers?
- Are there things you'd like to do more of?
- Are there things you'd like to do less of?
- What are the great things that you want to continue doing?
- Is there anything missing that you feel you could add in?

2 ENERGY EXCHANGE MAP

In my experience, driven people operating in the bad-stress zone have a tendency to withdraw and try to solve the issue themselves. Increased self-reliance is accompanied by a self-narrative of:

- 'No one else can help me with this.'
- 'I should be able to cope.'
- 'I'm a strong person. I can do this.'
- 'This is ridiculous. I don't need any help; I just need to pull myself together.'

If any of this self-talk is sounding familiar, then this exercise is a particularly important one for you.

Take a blank sheet of paper and work through the following steps:

- Write your name in the centre of the page.
- In a circle around your name, write the names of all the people you interact with on a regular basis.
- For each person who supports you or you get positive energy from, draw an arrow from that person towards your name in the centre. (The more support/positive energy you get, the thicker the arrow you draw.)
- For each person who you give support to and/or who drains your energy, add a line going the other way – from your name out to theirs. (Note: for many people, you'll have arrows going in both directions, but their thickness may differ.)
- Add any new people who come to mind and repeat the process.

4   Looking at your map, who are the people where the energy exchange feels good? Draw a circle round their name.

5   Looking at your map, who are the people where the energy exchange feels off kilter? Draw a square around their name.

You'll end up with something that looks like this:

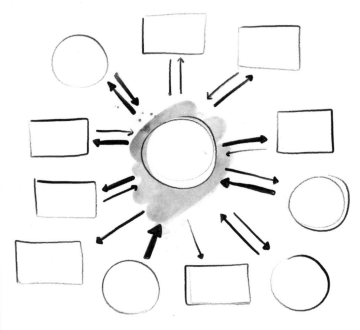

Energy exchange map

EXERCISE REVIEW

Looking at your map, consider the following questions:

- What do you notice about the ratio of energy given versus energy received?
- What do you notice about the amount of time you are spending with positive energy people versus energy drainers?
- Based on what you now know, is there anything you would like to change?
- Write down the names of those people you have circled. These people make up your support team. I'll be referring to them as we move through the rest of the programme.

Names of the people in my support team are:

_____

_____

_____

_____

_____

HELPERS THAT COULD BECOME HINDERERS

The coping strategies you outlined in the stress helpers exercise on pages 41 and 42 have got you to where you are today, and that's great. Even so, you may be living with a nagging feeling that there is something out of line, and your stress-relieving strategies aren't working as well as they used to. It can be frustrating and unsettling when things that have served us well for much of our life start to have unintended consequences. This shift over time is normal; our bodies have stored the experiences of our lives as we have moved through our careers. As our bodies and minds change as we get older, they react differently to the next waves of stress (good or bad).

The information in the section, together with the exercises, will help you take another look at your stress helpers and identify which of them have a potential dark side and could actually become hinderers.

- Helpers: strategies that nourish and sustain your success.
- Hinderers: strategies that may have unintended consequences and actually reduce your capacity to succeed.

You may think the above is obvious but, as you work through this chapter, you'll see it's not that simple. Whatever choices you end up making, it's important to remember you are human and there is no perfect world. It's simply not possible for us to consistently make the choices that will help us. In fact, feeling guilty about making hindering choices can actually contribute to the stress response itself! I therefore encourage an 80/20 approach:

- 80% of the time, make choices that will help you maintain and sustain your performance.

- 20% of the time, make different choices if you need to. Sometimes we just want to do something that we know isn't great for our body and/or mind in the medium term, but in the short term is hugely (and compellingly) attractive and enjoyable.

My objective here is to give you information about those helpers that have the potential to become hinderers. With this information you can make your own choices. There is no value in preaching and telling you what you should be doing. You and your set of circumstances are unique – and so should your choices be.

I have structured the information offered here into the following categories:

- Food and nutrition
- Activity and movement
- Fluids

FOOD AND NUTRITION

This can be one of those subjects which causes an involuntary eye-roll and makes people throw their arms up in the air. One day, research tells us that chocolate and wine are good for us, the next day, they're public health enemy number one. What I offer you here is my personal experience of researching, experimenting and testing different nutrition approaches.

I started to become interested in nutrition as my digestive and gut issues got steadily worse over a 10-year period. For example, I regularly experienced very uncomfortable pain under my ribs on my right side. The pain would be so uncomfortable in some meetings I'd have to stand up to move and stretch to try to relieve it (very ungainly). I would be very ill after eating mildly fatty foods combined with normal amounts of red wine (half a bottle or so). With the help of my doctor, we explored every possible medical cause. I believed these things needed a 'diagnosis' so I could find a solution to cure the underlying problem(s) and move on. We explored gluten intolerance (I was tested twice for coeliac disease), gall bladder issues, anaemia and bowel cancer. Thankfully, none of these came back as being medically diagnosable. So, getting desperate, I started to research nutrition. I've collaborated with a number of experts and nutritionists over the years, and in particular with one notable expert who transformed my understanding of my body's response to food as a result of stress levels. In collaboration with that expert, Rebecca Jones of Inspired Wellbeing, I have noted in the table below the likely effect on your body and mood of common habits we slip into as a result of our busy lives.

Choices	Likely effect	
	Body	**Mind**
High amounts of sugar	Cause spikes and increase in blood sugar and insulin, contribute to weight gain, link to type 2 diabetes, increase sugar cravings, feed less beneficial bacteria and fungus, can increase Candida overgrowth and lower immunity.	Activate the reward centre of the brain, can be highly addictive, can slow cognitive function, and can lower mood, increase anxiety and sadness.
Increased salt	Increases the amount of water present, which can then increase blood pressure and create a strain on the arteries, heart, kidneys and brain. Disrupts the gut/ immune response.	Causes cognitive defects.
Too much saturated fat	Can increase cholesterol and lead to weight gain. Can be linked with heart disease.	Decreases cognition.
Insufficient beneficial fats (mono-unsaturated, poly-unsaturated, essential fatty acids)	Can cause inflammation, creaky joints, dry/cracking/ scaly skin, dry eyes, constipation, hormonal imbalance and can increase allergies.	Decrease cognition, leads to low mood/ depression or other mental health issues, anxiety and fat cravings.

Choices	Likely effect	
	Body	**Mind**
Lots of processed meats	Increase blood pressure (salt), increase toxins (processing and chemicals), can lead to weight gain and constipation and increase risk of bowel and stomach cancer and heart disease.	Additives and preservatives can be toxic to the brain affecting its function, increasing cravings and inflammation.
Processed ready-meals	Increase sugar and salt levels (see above), can cause slow bowel movements linked to low fibre, can increase blood sugar and insulin, increase inflammation, lower immunity and increase nutrient deficiency.	Increase cravings, decrease mood and cognitive function.
Low vitamin D	Increases the risk of soft bones, osteoporosis and bone pain. Can lower immunity, contribute to hormone imbalance, lead to a higher risk of cardio-ovascular disease, and has links with autoimmune diseases.	Can be linked to depression and higher levels of anxiety, higher risk of dementia/ Alzheimer's disease and other neurological problems.

Choices	Likely effect	
	Body	Mind
Starchy white carbohydrates	Similar effects to sugar; can spike blood sugar and insulin levels increasing the risk of diabetes. Increase cravings, increase appetite, leading to weight gain. Link with Candida overgrowth in the gut.	Increase mood highs and lows. Linked to depression, impaired focus/concentration.
Not enough fibre	Increases constipation from lack of fibre, increases inflammation, can have an effect on hormone balance and can increase risk of bowel cancer.	Linked to higher levels of anxiety and stress response – relating to inflammation in the gut and lack of fibres that feed beneficial bacteria.
Skipping meals	Drops in blood sugar can lead to binge eating. Weight gain through slowing of metabolism.	Can cause impaired focus, irritability, anxiety, increased hormone production of cortisol – stress response.
Eating late	Can lead to weight gain, higher blood sugar and insulin and increases risk of diabetes, indigestion/heart burn.	Can result in restless sleep, disturbing dreams and impair memory/cognition.

There are deliberately no amounts or guidelines in the table above, as every one of us has a different constitution. What is too much for one person may be OK for another. It's your body. Make the choices that feel right for you. If you want to get into more specifics for your personal biological make-up and circumstances, investing in a few sessions with a qualified nutritionist is well worth it. Look for someone with a diploma or degree qualification and an affiliation with a nutritional board such as BANT (British Association for Nutrition and lifestyle Medicine), CNHC (Complementary and Natural Healthcare Council) or the FNTP (Federation of Nutritional Therapy Practitioners). Once you've made a shortlist, contact one or two people to find out about their approach and experience. A relationship with a nutritionist is very personal so it is important that you feel they understand your individual needs.

We looked earlier at the principle of making nourishing choices – giving helpers 80% of the time, leaving room for that 20% when we want to enjoy things that may not be that helpful to us in the long term. However, even with the best intentions, within that 80% we can often experience cravings for certain foods. Sometimes when you crave something it is genuinely because your body needs it, or your physiology is in a particular state. For example, inadequate mineral levels can produce salt cravings; pregnancy increases certain hormone levels producing varying cravings. Aside from these physiological craving triggers, we are often drawn to making choices that could be hinderers to our wellbeing due to either habit or emotional avoidance.

- Some nutritional cravings are actually just choices that have become habitual, or even ritualistic. For example, having a flat-white coffee in the morning or having that 'well-deserved' gin and tonic when you get home from work. You may also have strong associations of particular foods or drink with certain events.

- Alternatively, a craving can appear because you are (subconsciously) trying to avoid thinking or feeling. Don't skip this point and think you never do this... your brain may be deceiving you into not recognising this in yourself. Using food and/or drink to avoid/dampen down emotion is actually very common, but why does it work? Well, while your brain is immensely complex, it also has some lovely simplicity that comes into play here. Food and drink use most of your five senses (see, hear, feel, touch, taste). Neuroscience tells us that if you use just one of your five senses, your brain will be taken away from active thought, even if for just a brief moment. This knowledge is a big part of the principles underpinning yoga, meditation and mindfulness, where you are encouraged to tune into your senses to help calm your racing brain.

In relation to nutrition, the behaviour of using food or drink to avoid emotion is often called 'emotional eating'. Given that the distraction away from our thoughts when using our senses only lasts for a short amount of time, we continue eating or drinking either to continue to numb thought, or out of habit. The trouble is, the concept of emotional eating is usually associated with people who struggle to manage their weight, so you may not have applied it to your own situation. Indeed, you could be outwardly very healthy but still be making hindering choices based on a habit of emotional avoidance.

I regularly come back to this thinking when experiencing a craving. For example, I might come home after a full day of work and crave a glass of red wine. My choice is not to drink during the week, so this craving is annoying. Resisting cravings usually makes us want them more. A modern adaptation of one of Carl Jung's theories is that 'what you resist, persists'. Thus, rather than trying to stop or resist the craving, I think about what else is going on that may be drawing me to it. I don't generally drink during the week, so it's not a habit. It must therefore be some sort of emotional avoidance. I ask myself the following:

- What's happened during the day (or preceding days) that I don't want to address?
- Is there something coming up that I'm anxious about?
- Has someone irritated me, and I haven't said what I wanted to say about that?

After working on understanding my cravings over time, I can now identify the triggers for most of them. Switching from resistance to noticing is usually enough to eliminate the craving itself. However, if noticing doesn't help, I choose an alternative to satisfy it – an alternative that is a helper. I'll share these later on.

FLUIDS

If you are an adult male, your body is 55–60% water. As an adult female, you are roughly 50–55% water[7]. You probably already know that staying hydrated is essential to our well-being, but it's always worth a reminder of why this is so important.

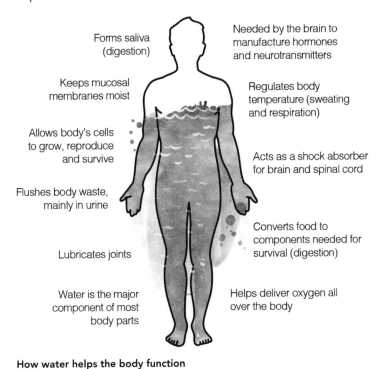

Forms saliva (digestion)

Keeps mucosal membranes moist

Allows body's cells to grow, reproduce and survive

Flushes body waste, mainly in urine

Lubricates joints

Water is the major component of most body parts

Needed by the brain to manufacture hormones and neurotransmitters

Regulates body temperature (sweating and respiration)

Acts as a shock absorber for brain and spinal cord

Converts food to components needed for survival (digestion)

Helps deliver oxygen all over the body

How water helps the body function

---

7   Grodner, M., Escott-Stump, S. and Dorner, S. (2015) *Nutritional Foundations and Clinical Applications: A Nursing Approach*, 6th Edition, Mosby

In recent years, this awareness has inspired many of us to carry water bottles around with us, to monitor how much we are drinking. As a side note, if you use a plastic water bottle, please make sure it is BPA free[8] or, even better, not plastic at all, but stainless steel or glass.

How much you drink is a good thing to pay attention to. Many years ago, I can remember times when I was so engrossed in the buzz of my work that I literally didn't eat or drink for hours on end. I even ignored my body's call to visit the bathroom. I'd think about taking a quick break then notice another email, or someone would come and ask me something – so that came first. Rather than being aware of the strain this was putting on my body and the adverse effect it was having on my cognitive abilities, I saw it as a strength – it meant I was so productive! I could keep going for so long.

So how much fluid do you need? The most commonly quoted figure is that we need two litres of fluid a day. However, the amount your body needs is unique to you. Factors that impact how much you need are: weight, gender, ambient temperature, diet, level of exertion and, yes, you guessed it, levels of stress.

To calculate how much fluid your body needs multiply your weight in pounds by 0.66. This will give you your answer in fluid ounces[9]. If you want to convert fluid ounces to litres, multiply by 0.03. Make a note of your result.

---

8   What is BPA and why is it bad for you?: https://www.medicalnewstoday. com/articles/221205.php

9   https://www.slenderkitchen.com/article/how-to-calculate-how-much-water-you-should-drink-a-day

> *In normal circumstances, my daily water goal is:*
>
>
>
> *Note: your total daily water goal includes water you get from food.*

Using this formula, my daily fluid goal is 2.8 litres
(141 x 0.66 = 93 fluid ounces. 93 x 0.03 = 2.79 litres)

An average person, eating a well-balanced and healthy diet, will get approximately 20% of their daily fluid from food. I'm pretty average in build so my target intake matches the most commonly quoted figure. However, I know that if I am spending time in the bad-stress zone, I need to drink more. Also, being of fair complexion, I need significantly more than two litres a day in hot climates. For the last eight or so years I have really paid attention to my fluid intake and, now, if there are days where I am busier and more focused, I can really feel if I haven't had enough. Two litres felt like a lot to start with, but now feels normal.

Remember, you will need to increase your fluid intake when you are more active, stressed or in a hotter/dryer climate than you are used to. Dry climates include air-conditioned environments, especially those of aircraft cabins where the air is around 12% humidity[10] (drier than you will find in most deserts).

A note of caution: over hydrating can actually be damaging. It would be remiss of me not to point this out, but don't worry too much as you need to drink a very large amount of fluid in a very short amount of time to get into the danger zone.

---

10 https://www.telegraph.co.uk/travel/travel-truths/why-are-planes-so-cold/

Over hydration can cause hyponatremia, which is when sodium in blood becomes too diluted. Symptoms include confusion, headaches, nausea and bloating. These are often things that are confused with dehydration. In severe cases, hyponatremia can lead to seizures, organ failure and even death.

Fluids in food

If you eat a well-balanced diet, you'll get about 20% of your total fluid requirement from food. I wouldn't get too obsessive about this, but it's worth recognising those foods that have the highest water content. I've listed them in the table below. In my experience, when we are busy, these are not the foods we typically reach for. Thus, if we haven't got time to drink water *and* we're not eating hydrating foods, it's a double whammy.

Food	Water content (%)[11]
Lettuce	96
Celery	95
Cucumber	95
Courgette/zucchini	94
Tomatoes	94
Watermelon	92
Bell peppers	92
Cauliflower	92
Strawberries	91
Cantaloupe melon	90
Peaches	89
Oranges	88
Plain yoghurt	88
Cottage cheese	80

11 https://www.healthline.com/nutrition/19-hydrating-foods#section1

Water

We are incredibly fortunate in the developed world to have ready access to clean water. However, the quality of tap water is ever changing. It varies from place to place, season to season and house to house. Tap water is treated with a large number of chemicals in order to kill bacteria and other microorganisms. In addition, it may contain other undesirable contaminants.

Typical tap water includes[12]:

- chlorine
- fluorine compounds
- trihalomethanes (THMs)
- salts of: arsenic, radium, aluminium, copper, lead, mercury, cadmium, barium
- hormones
- nitrates
- pesticides.

All of the above place extra stressors on our body. So, if you are experiencing prolonged periods of bad stress, part of your strategy to nourish your body could be to drink the cleanest water possible. To avoid the scourge of water in single-use plastic bottles (often also with BPA), I would recommend you buy a water filter. These vary vastly in cost from a low-cost filter jug through to a built-in system that delivers filtered water through your tap.

Caffeinated drinks (coffee, tea, energy drinks, etc.)

Caffeine gets a lot of attention in studies on health and wellbeing and is one of those things we seem to get conflicting advice on. Should I have none or some? How much is some? How much is too much? My objective is to give you what I

---

12 http://www.freshlysqueezedwater.org.uk/waterarticle_watercontent.php

consider to be the most useful information from a plethora of sources. From this, you can then make the choices that are right for you.

Caffeine is a naturally-occurring chemical found in the leaves, beans and fruits of more than 60 plants. It is also classed as a stimulant drug, which means it speeds up the messages travelling between the brain and the body. Caffeine stimulates the central nervous system and wards off drowsiness by suppressing adenosine levels. (Adenosine is a molecule that serves as the 'energy currency' for your body's various cellular functions.) Caffeine blocks adenosine receptors in your brain[13], stopping that sleepy signal and perking you up.

Caffeine is considered to be the most commonly used psychoactive drug in the world[14] and can be naturally found in:

- Coffea arabica (coffee)
- Thea sinensis (tea)
- Cola acuminata (used as a nut, tea or in soft drinks including cola)
- Theobroma cacao (cocoa and chocolate)
- Paullinia cupana (used as guarana in snack bars and energy drinks).

Caffeine has many effects on the brain and body, some of which are desirable and positive (for example, increased alertness in the short term). The theme of us all being unique continues here. Each one of us has a personal and different reaction to, and tolerance for, caffeine. And even our own experiences will change depending on other factors (for example, levels of stress). In terms of nourishing your success, it's important to

13 http://bonhamchemistry.com/wp-content/uploads/2012/01/Caffeine_and_Adenosine.pdf
14 https://www.medicinenet.com/caffeine/article.htm

reflect on your own reactions to caffeine and be aware of the long-term effects of its overuse. The word 'use' is deliberate here. If you think of caffeine as a drug, it can assist in changing your relationship with it.

The following facts are based on research by James Lane, an emeritus professor of psychiatry at Duke University School of Medicine in Durham[15]:

- It can take between 8 and 12 hours for the body to eliminate the caffeine from one cup of coffee.
- Women who are on the oral contraceptive pill may keep caffeine in their system up to four hours longer than women who aren't.
- For regular caffeine users, waking up feeling groggy, confused or with a headache can be normal. These feelings are withdrawal symptoms from yesterday's coffee; symptoms which are relieved when they get their morning fix of caffeine. A vicious cycle.
- Caffeine can amplify stress in people who consume it every day. In a small study of habitual coffee drinkers, Lane found that caffeine amplifies the stress response in the body, resulting in increases in blood pressure and heart rate, as well as increases in the production of stress hormones.
- Professor Lane's research found that caffeine directly affects not only the way a person's body responds to stress, but also how the mind responds. Caffeine can magnify an individual's perception of stress.
- An exaggerated stress response can make a difference to people with conditions such as high blood pressure and type 2 diabetes. Lane encourages people with these

---

15 https://www.livescience.com/56603-interesting-facts-about-caffeine.html/

conditions, as well as people with prediabetes or border-line hypertension who are not yet on medication, to try eliminating coffee and other caffeinated beverages to see if it lowers their blood pressure or blood sugar levels.

I remember at a particularly busy time in my career using caffeine a lot to keep me going, even though I was aware of my body's heart rate increasing and feeling slightly 'outer worldly'. One particular occasion that sticks in my mind was driving to a crucial pitch presentation with a colleague. We'd been up late the night before and had had an early start to get to the pitch venue. We stopped at some motorway services, and my colleague ran in to get coffee. He returned, gleefully announcing that he'd got us a triple-shot each to get us going for the pitch. The sensible part of my brain told me not to drink it, but the part of my brain that wanted to win the pitch thought it might help give me the extra spark of energy I felt was lacking. I drank it. Thirty minutes later we were in with the client. My heart was racing and I was sweating. I could hear my voice as I presented – it was much faster than usual and had a slightly higher pitch. I tried to control my pace and managed to be coherent. What I couldn't control, however, were my hands, which had started visibly and quite violently shaking, and my skin, which I could feel was red and hot. It must have been obvious as the client actually expressed concern, asking if I was OK. I explained and made a joke of it and we all laughed. But it was an embarrassing and very unpleasant experience. I have been very careful in my use of caffeine since. For me, one shot is my maximum and I never have that after 2 pm or I can't sleep. And if I'm in the bad-stress zone, caffeine is a no-no.

Three to four shots (400mg[16]) of coffee a day is widely accepted as being the threshold for 'overuse'. Regular, long-term overuse can contribute to the following[17]:

- Nervousness
- Difficulty sleeping
- Restlessness
- Irritability and headaches
- Dizziness and ringing in the ears
- Muscle tremor
- Weakness and fatigue
- Rapid heart rate and quickened breathing rate
- Poor appetite, nausea, vomiting and diarrhoea
- Increased thirst, frequent urination or increased urine volume
- Irregular heart rate or rhythm
- Low blood pressure with faintness or falls

I now look at the research available on the effects of caffeine and can see that I was experiencing many of the symptoms of overuse; and that overuse was happening when my body was already massively overstimulated through being in the zone of bad stress for long periods of time.

Remember also that many drinks (and other products) have widely varying amounts of caffeine in them, so always check the label. Here are some guidelines and examples of common caffeinated drinks[18]:

---

16 https://www.healthline.com/health/caffeine-effects-on-body#2
17 https://adf.org.au/drug-facts/caffeine/
18 Adapted from Food Regulation Standing Committee, Caffeine Working Group (2013) *The Regulation of Caffeine in Foods*, Australia and New Zealand

Product	Average caffeine content (mg/100ml)
Coffee, from ground coffee beans, espresso style	194.00
Coffee, cappuccino	101.90
Coffee, flat white	86.90
Coffee, long black	74.70
Red Bull®	32.00
Brewed black tea	22.50
Mountain Dew®	15.00
Brewed green tea	12.10
Coca Cola®*	9.70
Diet Coke®*	9.70
Coke Zero®*	9.60

* The Coca-Cola Company. (2015) Caffeine: Your Questions Answered[19]

Carbonated sugary drinks

I'm going to come down pretty hard on this source of fluid intake. I don't think there is any argument left in favour of choosing these as a source of fluid intake. Occasionally, fizzy drinks/sodas are fine; however, there is now so much research available to support a decision to avoid them. And I am not just talking about sugar-laden fizzy drinks, I'm also talking about those that are diet or low sugar. Consider the following: people who drink more than one fizzy soft drink a day are up to 60% more likely to develop obesity and high blood pressure,

19 https://www.coca-colacompany.com/stories/0000014b-079f-da6b-ad6f-6fdf6be40000

leading to heart attacks and strokes[20]. This level of consumption can also increase infertility for both sexes[21].

In guiding you to make nourishing choices, I want to draw the link between stress and sweetened fizzy drinks (whether sweetened with sugar or aspartame or similar). A recent study showed that while consuming sugar can alleviate short-term psychological stress, it causes long-term physical stress to your brain[22]. Long-term high sugar intake puts stress on, and negatively affects, the hippocampus. This is the area of the brain we looked at earlier in this chapter. It forms an important part of the limbic system, the region that regulates emotion and memory (in particular, long-term memory). It also plays an important role in spatial navigation.

As for aspartame or other artificial sweeteners, they mimic the effects of sugar outlined above, but may also come with added downsides (ranging from allergies to liver damage and cancer). There is an ongoing debate about whether these artificial sweeteners are fit for human consumption and in what doses. As with so many relatively recent food innovations, we probably don't know the full story. My view is that if governments and health bodies are investigating and researching the effects, it must mean there is enough base level concern to justify research funding. Given that, my choice is to avoid this category of fluid entirely.

---

20 Ravi Dhingra, Ramachandran Vasan and colleagues in Boston, Massachusetts, USA. Study into the association between soft drink consumption and the risk of metabolic syndrome

21 https://www.bu.edu/sph/2018/02/13/one-or-more-soda-a-day-could-decrease-chances-of-getting-pregnant/

22 https://www.ncbi.nlm.nih.gov/pubmed/25879513

Alcohol

As with sugar and caffeine, we are inundated with guidance on how much (if any) alcohol is good for us. Again, advice and research are often contradictory. Your choices on how to, or how not to, incorporate alcohol into your life are personal, but I do believe most people are now aware if they are consuming more than is healthy. Whether or not you use that awareness to change your behaviour is the issue in question here, and, again, my focus is looking at how you use alcohol in relation to your levels of stress.

A glass of wine in the evening might be fine to help you switch off and relax. However, if you are consuming large amounts of alcohol to try and deal with being in the bad-stress zone, you will feel like you are achieving some relief, but this is only short term. As with sugar intake, you are putting your body under significant physiological stress in the long term.

Alcohol has the opposite effect on the body to caffeine in that it is a depressant rather than a stimulant. It causes more adenosine to accumulate in your system, which brings on that sluggish, sleepy feeling. And we all know that it can also slow reaction times, reduce your balance and fine motor skills, and impair your cognition in a way that causes poor judgement[23]. The health downsides of alcohol abuse are well known too, with its affect largely being on the liver and brain.

So, in relation to managing your bad stress, alcohol is putting extra physiological stress on the parts of your body that are already overworking. It could be a contributory factor to some of the physiological and psychological catalysts you identified in Chapter 1.

---

23 https://www.cdc.gov/alcohol/faqs.htm#how

Choosing good quality fluids

Caffeine, sugary drinks and alcohol can all become part of our habitual way of managing stress. To break the habit, below are some alternatives that you may enjoy that will also nourish you, calm the cravings but still deliver your daily hydration.

Substitutes and alternatives	
Fluid	**Alternative choice**
Water	• Kefir (water or milk) • Fruit/vegetable-infused water (use a BPA-free infuser water bottle) • Fruit tea (read the ingredients – avoid teas with added sugar)
Caffeinated coffee	• Decaffeinated coffee • Rooibos tea (has quite a woody, smoky taste so can work as a coffee replacement) • Dandelion root or chicory root coffee
Carbonated drinks (whether diet or full sugar)	• Kombucha (a fermented, lightly effervescent sweetened black or green tea drink – has the benefit of being a probiotic, too) • Carbonated water (flavoured as plain water above if you wish) • Milk (not flavoured – as that involves sugar)
Spirits	There are some very good non-alcoholic spirits available now, and it's a growing market so we'll have much more choice as time moves on. Seedlip® is my go-to alternative to replace a gin and tonic.
Beer	There are some very good low or zero alcohol beers available. Becks blue is a favourite among my friends when they don't want alcohol.

Substitutes and alternatives	
Fluid	**Alternative choice**
Wine	I've not yet found a red or white wine substitute that I find palatable. There is an alcohol-free sparkling rosé called 'So Jennie' that tastes good, but is high in sugar at 7.5g per 100ml. So be aware of this if choosing it as one of your substitutes.

It can seem daunting thinking about things that currently don't take up mind-time for you. However, if you've identified any gut or bowel-related catalysts in Chapter 1, you need to pay attention to your nutrition. If you nourish your body, it will allow you to sustain your success naturally.

I have always had an interest in food. We had lots of Swiss cuisine growing up, and this was a challenge as a weight conscious teenager. Regular fayre included würßt of many different descriptions, rößti, fondue and a wide variety of creamy sauces that seem to be part of traditional Swiss cooking. Even a salad had to have a significant amount of dressing. All utterly delicious, but through most of my life, my concern was keeping my weight low rather than thinking about nutrition. Once I left home and had more control over what I ate, I followed the pundit's advice that fat and sugar were the main things to avoid. In times of stress I used to grab what was most convenient and low fat. I would go for ready-made flavoured rice to shove in the microwave, low-fat yoghurts, packets and packets of processed ham and chicken (protein is good for you right?) and lots of fruit salads with honey (not realising that even natural sugar can be a problem if not eaten with longer chain carbohydrates). For over 20 years my gut and bowel issues got worse and worse.

I had three major catalysts that ultimately led to me having to accept responsibility for what was happening to my body. The first one was that incident on the motorbike. The second was a year later, when my husband had his most manic episode to date. At that point I realised I had to leave the marriage for my own safety and sanity. The third catalyst was three years after my divorce when my body and mind wouldn't let me continue operating at the pace I was at, and I was signed off work, needing a full break of three months before returning.

In taking responsibility, I started to research more and more and for the first time accepted the mind-body connection. I started to see how my symptoms were exacerbated by the combination of a demanding job, the increasingly stressful home environment and the 'helper' choices I was making. My natural drive and the additional stress of my home life meant that I was living with consistently elevated levels of cortisol and adrenaline, directly affecting my physiology. In retrospect, even without the stress of living with someone with bipolar disorder, I think I would have ended up in the same situation. My drive was just too strong to allow me to stop and take stock. Through research, I realised I could make changes and help my body get back to being fully functional, thereby supporting my mind and my drive for success. I read books and listened to podcasts, I went on yoga and nutrition retreats, I tried different combinations of foods and I used supplements to help rebuild my gut bacteria. I am now, for the first time in 20 years, at a point where my body is fully functioning, and I understand how to fuel and nourish it. It took five years of focus to get to this point. I used my drive to focus on understanding how to nourish my success, rather than looking at success itself.

In the tables below, I've shared with you some of the things that have worked for me. They may be useful for you, too, but do remember you are unique. I recommend finding a nutritionist to support you (using the guidance provided earlier). You may need three to five sessions or more, over a two-year period, then one a year after that to check in. It's not a huge investment given the payoff.

These tables summarise my learning and they're something I often refer back to. I aim to stick to these for 80% of the time (remember the 80/20 principle).

Craving	My substitutes/options
Something sweet	• Reach for one Medjool date (no more as high in fructose) or a handful of berries, a clementine or a kiwi (low fructose fruit). Eat them slowly! • Have some dark chocolate – one square (over 75% cocoa content)
Meat-based protein	• Meat substitute: tempeh – barbecue flavour = great sausage substitute • If meat, choose grass fed (not grain fed) • Don't eat meat late at night
Pasta/rice/ processed bread	• Sweet potato, nuts (unsalted), brown or wild rice • Lentils, quinoa, buckwheat • Celeriac or cauliflower steaks
An evening snack	• Don't eat after 9 pm • Savoury: 30 g of cheese (goats milk cheese preferably) with two sourdough crackers • Sweet: Greek yoghurt (full fat), a small amount of granola (low sugar) and half a banana

Craving	My substitutes/options
Alcohol	● Have a fermented drink in my favourite wine or spirits glass (e.g. kombucha or kefir). Add ice, lemon/lime (or other decoration) ● Seedlip® non-alcoholic spirit (a great gin replacement) ● 'So Jennie' (prosecco or champagne replacement)
Something salty (crisps, salted nuts)	● Trail mix (using unsalted nuts). Make at home with almonds, pumpkin seeds and sunflower seeds; dry fried with chosen spices ● Fresh popcorn (olive oil, pinch of salt, chilli flakes) ● Roasted chickpeas: Rinse chickpeas from a can, toss them in coconut oil, and bake at 160°C. Then toss with a mix of any low- or no-salt seasoning (e.g. curry powder, paprika, cumin)

Habit	My new habits
Too much coffee	● Have one coffee a day (and not after 2 pm)
Eating late	● Don't eat late! ● Leave at least two hours after eating before going to bed
Not enough water	● Use a plastic (BPA-free) or stainless steel water bottle to keep track of water consumption. Drink evenly throughout the day

Habit	My new habits
Not enough fibre	● Eat loads of cruciferous vegetables (broccoli, courgette, kale, spinach, cabbage, cauliflower, radish, watercress) ● Eat the above with every meal (including breakfast) ● Take a green powder supplement if not able to eat the vegetables (spirulina, chlorella, wheatgrass)

Nutrition choices awareness

This exercise will help you connect your nutritional choices with your underlying mood and levels of stress.

Complete the table on the worksheet in the following order:

- Column 1: list all of the cravings you can think of, then ask a few people who know you well what they see you reaching for when you are stressed.
- Column 2: identify which cravings are habits, and which might be emotional avoidance. If you find this difficult, think about it over time as those cravings arise. If you do identify any cravings that aren't habits, what emotions might be underlying the craving? (For example, feeling overwhelmed, exhausted, angry, frightened, bored, sad, lonely, etc.)
- Column 3: in which stress zone does the craving arise?
- Before completing the final column, look through your list of cravings and circle any that have the potential to be hinderers (draw on the knowledge you now have from this chapter).

- Column 4: for those cravings you have circled, complete the last column with choices you could try as substitutes or replacements.

Description of craving	Is the craving a habit or linked to emotional avoidance?	In which stress zone does the craving arise?	Substitute/ replacement

Over the course of the next month or so, experiment with your substitutes and replacements. Be open-minded as you try different things. If your mindset is 'I'll try it, but it won't work', guess what, it will never work! Try, fail, try again or try something else (with the same goal in mind). Keep your chart updated with the things you try. Remove things that don't work and try something different.

Pay attention to how the changes you are making affect the physiological catalysts you noted in Chapter 1. Where do you see improvements?

EXERCISE REVIEW

- What do you now know about your habits and cravings?
- On a scale of 1–10, how motivated are you to make the changes you've noted (10 = highly motivated; 1 = not motivated at all)?
- Who could you enlist from your support team map to help you achieve the changes you've noted?
- What specific requests do you have of the people in your support team to help you?

ACTIVITY AND MOVEMENT

I'm sure you already know how important activity and movement are to your health and wellbeing. At the beginning of this chapter, in the stress-relief strategies exercise on page 41, you will have identified how/if you use exercise as part of your life.

Historically, the main academic focus in assessing the benefits of exercise has been in how it affects our physiology. But, in recent years, there has been more exploration and understanding of how exercise can improve our mental health and wellbeing. In particular, how it can contribute to helping people beat depression, anxiety and other mental health challenges. Interestingly, there has been much less focus on what happens when we exercise while in extended periods of distress. There has also been less focus on the types of exercise we take when in distress, and their relative effects. This is the area I want to explore with you now. My intention here is to make you more aware how the type of exercise you choose may help or hinder your success, and how different choices will have different impacts depending on where you are on the stress curve.

High-intensity, endurance or extreme exercise

If you are driven and you love your exercise, you are likely to have a high degree of commitment towards the exercise you do. Many of the people I coach manage to balance a highly-demanding job with a vigorous exercise regime. Those regimes will often include competitive challenges such as Tough Mudder or 10k races through to ultra-marathons and ironmen/women competitions. When you are in the good-stress zone this is all fine, vigorous exercise is likely to be contributing to your feeling of being energised and your ability to focus. However, if you are in the bad-stress zone, you will have increased levels of cortisol and adrenaline in your body.

- Cortisol: Provided exercise sessions are not too strenuous and long, and nutritional needs are met, your body will control cortisol release. However, if you're already living with high levels of cortisol and adrenaline, high-intensity, endurance-type exercise will release even more cortisol.

- Adrenaline: Adrenaline increases the cardiorespiratory activity that facilitates exercise. It can improve your mood. Even the anticipation of exercise can spark a rush of adrenaline. During exercise, or before, your brain sends a signal to your adrenal glands. In response, your adrenal glands excrete adrenaline into the bloodstream. But, again, if you already have elevated levels of adrenaline in your body, high-intensity exercise will trigger more. And, crucially, the fitter you are, the less adrenaline is secreted, so the more you have to exercise to get the same 'hit'. This is where the expression 'adrenaline junkie' comes from. Perhaps this term brings bungee jumping, skydiving or other similar activities to mind. However, in reality, you could be an adrenaline junkie leading a relatively normal life. It's this adrenaline addiction that is worth watching out for, as it is often this that causes exercise to tip over into being a hindrance, rather than a helper.

How do you know if the type of exercise you are choosing is helping or hindering your success? Generally, getting high-intensity exercise at regular intervals during a week is recognised as being a good thing. However, consider your mindset in relation to your exercise: do you have a rough training plan, which you can adapt depending on the day/week you've had; or are you driven to stick to your plan and push yourself to do hard exercise even if you don't feel like it? If you're pushing yourself to train hard (perhaps with a competitive race or goal in mind) when your body is telling you otherwise, then your exercise strategy may be tipping into being a hindrance to your well-being in the medium to long term. If you're already operating in that distress zone, you now know that high-intensity exercise will extend the time your body is flooded with adrenaline and cortisol.

Another thing to pay attention to is your relationship with your exercise plan. Where are you on the scale of being committed to exercise or being dependent on it? Only you can know this. From my coaching work and personal experience, I believe we know instinctively when we cross that threshold into dependency.

I've always been committed to building activity and movement into my life. There was a significant period in my life when I let that slip. Once I rectified that I vowed I would never drop exercise again. However, after that and over a period of three or four years I shifted from just being committed to exercise to being dependent on it; I was using it as a distraction from my crumbling marriage, as a way of managing my work-related stress and as a way of maintaining what I can now recognise as an addiction to adrenaline. I was over-exercising by combining high-energy gym classes like Les Mills BodyAttack™ and Body-Pump™ with running and HIIT circuit training. These classes are great when chosen at times that our body can cope with the elevated stress response they create. However, I was a long way from thinking about that. I would often do an hour's run in the morning and a gym class after a long working day. I had

HIIT routines I could carry out in my hotel room and would book hotels with a gym when travelling with work. I didn't completely lack awareness of what I was doing and did try some lower energy classes like BodyBalance™ or BodyJam™, but they weren't hard enough – my mindset was, 'If I'm going to spend time exercising, I want to get maximum "benefit"'. In addition to the over-exercising, I wasn't eating nutritionally balanced meals, instead focusing on high protein, low carb and low fat. Over a number of years, all of this was a recipe for disaster, and all contributed to my eventual breakdown.

It wasn't until four years after my breakdown that I went on my first full-week yoga retreat. I'd been practising yoga for about six years at this point, but was still drawn to Vinyasa flow or Ashtanga yoga, the more intense versions of the discipline. The retreat was phenomenal and a turning point for me in my relationship with both food and exercise. The week was run at the Kaliyoga venue in Spain. We had a 90-minute Yin yoga practice morning and evening, with 30 minutes of meditation at the end of each practice. We enjoyed superb nutrient-dense meals, received nutritional advice and guidance, had time to relax as well as options to go hill walking in the stunning Alpujarras. I left that week with so much new knowledge. I had an epiphany in my understanding of fats in our diet. Having spent my whole adult life to that point believing all fat was bad, I now understood that we need good fats to help our bodies absorb nutrients, to fuel our muscles during exercise and promote satiation. Consuming too little fat as part of a weight-loss diet can actually create the physiological conditions that increase stress and anxiety[24]. I left the retreat knowing more about protein

24 www.psychologytoday.com/gb/articles/200304/the-risks-low-fat-diets

from non-animal sources (beans and pulses), and committed to eating way more dark green and cruciferous vegetables to aid food transition through, and cleansing of, the gut. I also left with a deep feeling of calm; partly due to the deep slow work of the Yin yoga. I recognised for the first time how gentle exercise had the potential to nourish me, alongside higher intensity forms of exercise.

Activity choices awareness

This exercise will help you connect with your activity choices and how they relate to your levels of stress.
Before completing this exercise, look back at your outputs from your:

- stress-identifier timeline
- stress-relief strategies.

1 Using the table in the worksheet, write down all the exercise types that you enjoy or would like to try.

2 For each type of exercise, write 'Yes' or 'No' against each stress zone based on your insight of when it is most beneficial for you to choose it.

3 Add any additional notes for yourself. These may be reminders of what to tell yourself to help you make the nourishing choice. For example, knowing what you now know from this chapter, what would you tell yourself next time you are about to choose a high-intensity workout when you're in a high level of distress?

Here's an extract from my table as an example:

Exercise type	Stress zone		
	Calm	Eustress	Distress
Running	Yes	Yes	No
Notes: things to remind myself of	Don't be tempted to run after a really tough stressful day. Remember that a power walk or yoga flow will give me the same benefits, without the extra physical stressors. If I can't convince myself to not run, do a shorter run (no more than 5k).		
Power walk	Yes/No	Yes	Yes
Notes: things to remind myself of	If in the calm zone, seek out hills to walk up to increase intensity of the walk. Remember how being in nature on a walk has additional benefits.		
Yoga	Yes	Yes	Yes
Notes: things to remind myself of	Remember, you can vary intensity and type of yoga to balance your mood. For example, choose more energising Ashtanga or Vinyasa flow if in calm zone or Hatha or Yin yoga if in distress.		
BodyAttack™	Yes	Yes	No
Notes: things to remind myself of	Be careful if you choose this when on the edge of bad stress. You know it is an intense class!		

EXERCISE REVIEW

Keep your worksheet for this exercise somewhere you can refer back to it easily. Whenever you are about to take some exercise, ask yourself:

- How am I feeling right now? What stress zone am I in?
- How am I likely to feel after the exercise session?
- If I am in distress, could I choose a form of movement that is less intense (for example, a power walk or yoga)? If your answer to this question is anything in the territory of, 'That's not real exercise/that's a waste of time', you could be in a dependent relationship with your high-intensity exercise. As I was.

HELPERS THAT WILL ALWAYS BE HELPERS

I wanted to give you some information on things you can turn to without having to think. The things in the next section are much less likely to have unintended consequences. Let's focus on the benefits of each.

Hobbies/interests

When we are driven and successful, we are mostly energised by our work. This can mean we make choices to prioritise work over other things. Look back at the wheel of focus map you completed in Chapter 1 on page 21. Were interests and hobbies something you wanted to spend more time on? If so, read on. If not, skip this short section.

There are many reasons why hobbies and interests are good for us. In relation to nourishing your overall success, I believe the following are the main benefits:

- Stress relieving: focusing on something you enjoy, and could get absorbed in, will move your brain away from the challenging things in your work life.
- Creativity: hobbies often involve some form of creativity. Using your brain in different ways can have knock-on benefits for how you think creatively around problems.
- Socialising: often hobbies will involve you being connected to a different group to your work colleagues and friends.
- Distraction: hobbies can give you something to turn to if you become bored. Driven people are often restless and feel a need to be doing something. So a hobby could offer you a replacement to constantly checking those emails.

Time with supportive family and friends

We all react differently to stress. Some people feel the need to be around other people, and others retreat into themselves. If you are one of the latter, be careful not to take this retreating into yourself too far. There are many studies to support the benefits of social interaction and talking to people. If you have an internal self-narrative of, 'No one can help. I need to sort this out by myself', then you may be at greater risk of increasing your stress through greater isolation. Look back at your support team map and think about the people you could reach out to.

Movement that nourishes the body and mind

We looked at the various types of exercise and how they relate to stress earlier in this chapter. Activities like yoga, Pilates and tai chi are all activities that benefit the body and mind by having similar benefits. When practising them, you will be focusing on your breath (making it deeper, longer and slower). This allows you to soften your muscles and clear your mind as you move through the poses. All of this focuses you into the present moment. I could write a whole book on how amazing yoga is and how it has supported me and helped nourish my success.

All of these gentle mind/body types of movement offer you the opportunity to calm a busy mind and a body that is potentially in fight or flight mode (depending on your level of stress). You'll hear yoga teachers in particular inviting you to take what you learn on the mat and bring it into your daily lives. This invitation applies to the ability to calm your fight or flight response. Using breathing to focus on the present moment is hugely beneficial. Simply breathing deeply into your abdomen can move the body back into its parasympathetic nervous system, otherwise known as the 'rest and digest' nervous system.

It will slow the heart rate and increase the flow of hormones to those areas that have been 'shut down' if you were operating in fight or flight mode.

You only need 20 minutes of this kind of exercise for you to feel these benefits. If you're a yoga newbie, I can't encourage you strongly enough to add it into your list of helpers. You can start at home. My favourite online yoga teacher by a mile is called Adriene and she has many tutorials on YouTube. You can search for beginner to advanced, and for yoga for different times (for example, there is a 20-minute 'Yoga For A Dull Moment' option). You'll find her by searching 'Yoga With Adriene'.

Mindfulness

Mindfulness is a state of awareness of your experience in the present moment – a state of awareness that carries no judgement on what that experience is. It has its roots in Buddhism and has come a long way from 'hippydom' to being a legitimate cognitive tool to help us deal with the frenetic pace of today's world. While mindfulness is not an activity as such, it is often arrived at by practising mindfulness meditation, yoga or other mindfulness-inducing activities.

In the past, mindfulness was often viewed with scepticism by the business community; something that was more appropriate for holistic enthusiasts and hippy types. But, today, the medical field stands behind it as a well-researched and successful tool to deliver significant psychological and physiological benefits. The National Institute for Health and Care Excellence, NHS Choices and the Mental Health Foundation have all acknowledged the benefits of mindfulness in leading a healthy, stress-managed life.

With the explosion of interest in mindfulness, there has been a proliferation in the ways we can access it. If it's something you want to consider as part of your helpers, there are two main ways of accessing help to develop your skill in practising mindfulness:

1 In-person mindfulness activities (for example, courses, retreats, workshops).

2 Digital mindfulness activities (easily accessible digital versions of mindfulness, which you can carry around in your pocket and access as and when you need).

I've tried many options over the years. During my experimentation, I found it difficult to find a way of practising that worked for me. I'd find myself starting with an online app, and then getting bored. I'd get the giggles during 'in-person' activities, or I'd find the voices used in the various digital options I tried deeply irritating. Then I saw Andy Puddicombe's TED talk, 'Ten Mindful Minutes' and discovered Headspace.com, of which he is co-founder. Headspace offers an app to bring mindfulness to people in a simple accessible way. Andy is the voice of all the guided meditations. I have been a Headspace convert and devotee for over five years now. I love it for these reasons:

- It has a superb structure to support learning a new practice.
- It's not patronising.
- You can choose the duration of your sessions and vary it as often as you like.
- There are hundreds of different options depending on where you want to focus your practice (sport, creativity, focus, anxiety, sleep, etc.) There are even options for children.
- Andy's voice is very easy on the ear, calm and encouraging.

If you are operating in the distress zone a lot of the time, I can't recommend mindfulness enough. Try it. Persevere and see what works for you. It's not easy. If you're driven and successful, you're likely to have a busy mind. Don't expect to empty your mind when you practise mindfulness; it's more about letting thoughts come and go so you can be in the present moment.

Being in nature

More than 55% of the world's population now live in urban areas; a proportion that is expected to increase to 68% by 2050[25]. While there are many benefits of urbanisation, it is also associated with increased levels of mental health issues, including anxiety[26]. In 2013, a significant study[27] of 100,000 people over two years found a significant increase in wellbeing where people have increased proximity to green space.

Being in nature can help you manage yourself out of the distress zone. Even if you live in a very urban area, there will be a park or some green space within reasonable access somewhere. I encourage you to seek out nature as often as you can as part of your routine to nourish your success. Taking a dog for a walk is a great way to get into nature if you need a purpose beyond just walking. And, if you don't have your own dog, there's always www.borrowmydoggy.com.

---

25 https://www.un.org/development/desa/en/news/population/2018-revision-of-world-urbanization-prospects.html

26 Peen, J., Schoevers, R. A., Beekman, A. T. and Dekker, J. (2010) 'The current status of urban-rural differences in psychiatric disorders', Acta Psychiatrica Scandinavica 121 (2):84–93, John Wiley & Sons

27 White, M. P., Alcock, I., Wheeler, B. W. and Depledge, M. H. (2013) Would You Be Happier Living in a Greener Urban Area? A Fixed-Effects Analysis of Panel Data, *Psychological Science* 24 (6):920–928

Here are the benefits you can enjoy by being in nature:

- Spending time hiking or resting in a forest can measurably lower your cortisol rate, heart rate and blood pressure[28].

- Exposing your bare skin to moderate sun can increase your levels of vitamin D. One of the properties of vitamin D is that it supports the health of the immune system, brain and nervous system (all vital in helping us deal with levels of distress).

- Fresh air. Indoor air is up to 70 times more contaminated than outdoor air due to the amount of chemicals (household products) and plastics we bring into our homes.

- Grounding. This is the principle that, if we don't come into direct contact with the earth, a positive charge can build up in our bodies – a charge that increases inflammation and decreases sleep. If you think about it, there is something very lovely about walking barefoot on the grass or on the sand on a beach. Something most of us probably did as children but do much less as adults. There is growing scientific evidence for this, with research suggesting that a disconnect with earth's surface electrons is a contributor to physiological disfunction[29]. Try walking barefoot in the grass next time you are outside and see how it feels.

Enough good quality sleep

More and more recent studies and books provide evidence of the benefits of restorative sleep and the risks of not getting

---

28 Park, B. J., Tsunetsugu, Y., Kasetani, T., Kagawa, T. and Miyazaki, Y. (2010) 'The physiological effects of *Shinrin-yoku* (taking in the forest atmosphere or forest bathing): evidence from field experiments in 24 forests across Japan', PMC

29 Journal of Environmental and Public Health 2012; 2012: 291541. Published online 2012 Jan 12. doi: 10.1155/2012/291541

enough sleep. As with many of these things that are always helpers, we know they are helpers due to decades of research. These are a couple of the most important things that are known about sleep:

- If you're regularly getting less than seven hours sleep a night, you're doing as much damage to your body as someone who regularly smokes or drinks alcohol to excess.
- Sleep-deprived people often don't recognise that they are sleep deprived. Their low levels of energy become the norm, and they don't make the connection between how the ongoing lack of adequate sleep has compromised their mental and physical capability (which includes the slow accumulation of ill health)[30].

Tips for improving sleep:

- Stop using devices within one hour of going to bed. Evening use of active electronic devices has a negative effect on sleep, circadian rhythms and morning alertness. Active devices are ones you can interact with (as opposed to passive devices like simple e-readers)[31].
- According to Lisa Meltzer, an education scholar for the National Sleep Foundation, if you wake regularly during the night, hiding your clock so you can't check the time will help you reduce your stress about being awake and contribute to you being able to fall back to sleep.

---

30 Walker, M. (2017) *Why We Sleep: The New Science of Sleep and Dreams*, Allen Lane
31 Gradisar, M., Wolfson, A. R., Harvey, A. G., Hale, L., Rosenberg, R. and Czeisler, C. A. (2013) 'The Sleep and Technology Use of Americans: Findings from the National Sleep Foundation's 2011 Sleep in America Poll', *Journal of Clinical Sleep Medicine*, 9(12):1291–1299

- Keep your room cool. The National Sleep Foundation recommends a temperature of between 15 and 20 degrees Celsius.

- Create an evening routine around sleep; a routine that signals to your body that you'll be going to bed. A warm shower, candles, lavender scent, relaxing music, etc. Your routine needs to last about an hour, and should avoid all nutritional stimulants (coffee, chocolate, alcohol, etc.) and active devices.

- Practise progressive relaxation. This involves slowly tensing and relaxing every muscle in your body, starting with your toes and working all the way up your body.

Pure helpers' review

This exercise will help you focus on shifting your behaviours towards strategies that are helpful.

The table on the worksheet is divided into the six categories of helpers explored in this chapter.

With one coloured pen, mark on your worksheet how happy you are with this helper now.

Choose another coloured pen to mark where you would like to shift to.

(10 = the amount of time I spend on this feels perfect; 0 = I don't spend any time on this.)

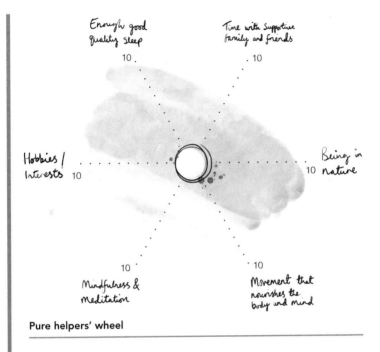

Enough good
quality sleep
10

Time with supportive
family and friends
. 10

Hobbies /
Interests 10

Being in
10 nature

10
Mindfulness &
meditation

10
Movement that
nourishes the
body and mind

Pure helpers' wheel

EXERCISE REVIEW

- Looking at the overall shifts you've noted and wish to make, what are your thoughts? Pay attention to both negative and positive thoughts, emotions (anger, sadness, guilt, frustration) and, if you can, capture what triggered those emotions.
- What do you now know about where you'd like to make choices to create more time for these helpers?
- On a scale of 1–10, how motivated are you to make the changes you've noted (10 = highly motivated; 1 = not motivated at all)?
- Who from your support team could help you achieve the changes you noted?
- What specific requests do you have of anyone in your support team? Go and ask them if they can help you.

REFLECTION

Building on the understanding of your catalysts, this chapter has given you a way of thinking about your stress, how you respond to different types of stress and the strategies you use to cope. To pull it all together, make a note of your insights and the areas you want to focus on.

Insights into my stress propensity and connection with physiological issues I am experiencing:

Looking at my stress timeline, I notice that...

The things I would like to focus on 80% of the time to help manage my stress and nourish my success are:

The things I'd like to pay attention to in my energy exchange with people are:

> *The things I'd like to pay attention to in my choices of nutrition are:*

> *The things I'd like to pay attention to in my choices of activity and movement are:*

> *The pure helpers I would like to cultivate are: (Remember these are helpers that don't have a dark side, and the potential to slip into being hinderers.)*

As you continue to work through this book – keep coming back to the worksheets from this chapter, adding in new insights around your coping strategies.

From this point forward, when you start to revert back to old habits, or start to drop your helpers because you are too busy, reflect and make notes (mental notes or in your notebook) as follows:

- What happens before I do something that doesn't nourish me? (Think about what happens minutes, hours and/or days before.)
- How can I hold the awareness of my trigger to use this hinderer so I can avoid it next time?

This reflection will help you notice your triggers to use hinderers and put you in a good position to make better choices that nourish you and sustain your success.

CHAPTER 3

INTRODUCTION

Having an open mind is a crucial part of being able to nourish your success. Carol Dweck referred to this openness as a 'growth mindset' in her bestselling book[32]. While her work is widely accepted and understood to help people learn through adopting a 'growth mindset', I extend the concept of openness more broadly to how you view your success, and your relationship with your drive. If you can't be open to hearing challenge, support, suggestion, criticism, encouragement, bad news or good news, it will be much harder for you to sustain and nourish your success. There are good and bad things we need to be open to. This is key. For those of us who are driven, we often find it hard to really hear the positive inputs we get or to celebrate things that have gone well. By the time something is done we are already pushing for the next thing – perhaps pushing on before acknowledging what was achieved (to ourselves or others). For me, being open is about being able to use all of your senses to continually challenge your current belief of what is right and how you operate. Being open is a key foundation to the skill of self-reflection. It is no accident that self-reflection plays a significant part in the exercises in this book. In her book *Reflective Practice* (2010), Gillie Bolton usefully defines self-reflection as: 'paying critical attention to the practical values and theories which inform everyday actions. This leads to developmental insight.'[33]

The focus of this chapter is to help you cultivate a mind that is as open as possible. You'll identify how open you currently

---

32 Dweck, C. S. (2006) *Mindset: The New Psychology of Success*, Random House
33 Bolton, G. (2010) *Reflective Practice, Writing & Professional Development*, SAGE

are and you'll get inputs, tools and exercises that will help you enhance your openness. By the end of this chapter, you'll have a series of thoughts to carry forward to the next chapter where we look at your insights. As you work through this chapter, try to resist the temptation to evaluate, judge or take action on the inputs and discoveries that come up; save that for Chapter 4 where you will start to consider which insights, if acted upon, will have the biggest impact in nourishing your success.

If you have any thoughts that are along the lines of 'I'm already open-minded, so I'm going to skim read/skip this chapter', then, guess what, you're not as open-minded as you think! I offer this challenge as I know it's something that the 'old me' would have thought at this point in the book. For those of us who have strong drive, finding the balance between being open versus believing our view is right is a tough one. I thought I'd always been good at admitting when I'm wrong or had made mistakes. When things inevitably went wrong as my company pushed the boundaries of digital integration, colleagues would comment how nice it was to work with a leader who didn't play the blame game. We got stuck in to fix the problems, and then learnt from what had happened. That's being open. I would get comments from other senior colleagues (mostly men) about how I led with no ego and had a strong capability to see the other person's point of view. That's being open too. However, what I now recognise is that while I could be open much of the time, I wasn't ready or able to be open most of the time. Much of the time to most of the time – a small but significant shift. My drive to succeed would convince me that my view of the world was the right one, and I would sometimes use all my energy to convince everyone I was right. I wouldn't give up. Sometimes that's a great quality. Sometimes it's not. Being open means still having the ability to hear a different view, even (and perhaps most importantly) in the midst of that utterly compelling belief that you are right.

One very funny but embarrassing moment of realisation about my sometime lack of openness came from Andrew, a colleague with whom I had worked for around five years. We were discussing his rail-commute to work from Cardiff to Bristol. I already knew this was how he got to work, and that to get to the office meant crossing the River Severn. Andrew mentioned one day he would be late into work for a few weeks as the tunnel under the river had works on it. My reaction was instant. Tunnel? Under the River Severn? I knew there were two bridges, but a tunnel? I'd grown up on the south coast in the UK and, as my father was an architect, there was lots of family discussion around the plans for the channel tunnel. Given this, I believed that if there was a tunnel somewhere else in the UK that connected land mass to land mass I would know. I queried Andrew with a very strong disbelief… to which he responded with a deep sigh. 'Janine, I come to work by a train that goes under the River Severn. Your questions aren't coming from a place of interest about something you don't know. They're coming from a place of not believing you could be wrong.' Ouch!

YOUR VIEW OF THE WORLD

You have a unique view of the world. And so does everybody else. Your view is based on your unique experience of getting to this point in your life. Believing your view of the world is right by definition suggests that you believe an alternative view is wrong. The alternative view could come from a number of different places; for example, another person, an organisation, a country or a decision.

When you believe you are right, you are looking through your own unique lens of the world, but the fact is, no one else will ever see or experience the same situation in exactly the same way as you do. Ever.

Ladder of inference

This model is a useful way of helping you understand how your unique experience of life is stored in your brain so efficiently that it creates your instant reaction to things that happen every day. Understanding this can help you recognise where you might be firmly believing your view is the right one when, in actual fact, your brain has just chosen to present you with that view. This model was first proposed by Chris Argyris, a former professor at Harvard Business School in the 1970s and later used by Peter Senge in his book *The Fifth Discipline: The Art & Practice of the Learning Organization*[34]. His model is called 'the ladder of inference'.

Before I share the detail of the model with you, I'd like to tell you a story. As you read it, I'd like you to imagine you are in the same situation and pay attention to what's going on in your mind (i.e. tune in to your inner voice).

---

34 Senge, P. M. (2006) *The Fifth Discipline: The Art & Practice of the Learning Organization*, 2nd Edition, Random House

> It's a November evening in Bristol around 5pm and I am driving my three-year-old niece back home. It's a miserable, dark, cold and wet winter evening. The route home takes me through an area of town that has a very bad reputation for drugs and violence. As I drive, my car makes an unusual shuddering noise and the engine dies. I manage to drift over to the side of the road and put my hazard lights on. I consider my options. My mobile is out of battery. There aren't any public pay phones around. I don't know anyone in this part of town. The windows are starting to fog up, but I can see a figure swaggering towards me, hands in pockets, hood up. The figure approaches my car and comes up to the door on the passenger side...

Let me stop there – what are you thinking right now? Without reading back over the story, just answer these questions based on what's at the front of your mind:

- How are you feeling (i.e. what's your empathetic reaction to my situation)?
- Where is the child sitting in the car?
- What do you know about the figure approaching the car? Gender? Clothing? Anything else?
- Have you imagined yourself doing anything as the figure approaches the car (for example, locking the doors, checking the windows are shut)?

Re-read the facts I gave you in the story. That's all you have and yet you've added all the details you noted above. Where did all of that come from? Well, that right there is your ladder of inference in action. The ladder visualises the process that our brains go through to reach a decision or action; and it happens in the blink of an eye without us being aware of it.

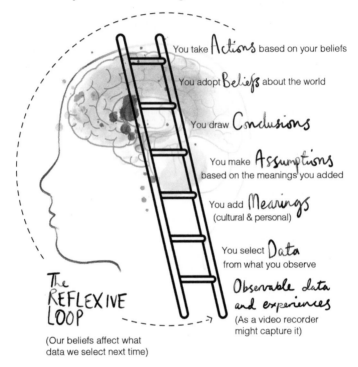

You take **Actions** based on your beliefs

You adopt **Beliefs** about the world

You draw **Conclusions**

You make **Assumptions** based on the meanings you added

You add **Meanings** (cultural & personal)

You select **Data** from what you observe

Observable data and experiences (As a video recorder might capture it)

The **REFLEXIVE LOOP**

(Our beliefs affect what data we select next time)

Ladder of inference: based on Chris Argyris and Peter Senge's work

If you think back to the story and now look at the ladder of inference above, you can start to see how your brain is adding so much to the observable experiences (or facts). Your brain is so fast at making judgements that you will see these additions as facts when they are actually just a version of reality created by your own ladder of inference.

Now look at the reflexive loop in the model; you can see how, if you chose to lock the doors, you would reinforce your belief that you were safe *because* you locked the doors. So, next time, in a similar situation, the meaning and assumption in the ladder would deliver the same conclusion and action.

One other point to note is that your world view isn't only informed by your personal experiences; it's also informed by what you hear from friends and family, what you see and consume in the media and anything else that floats your way.

Strength of belief in your view of the world

A strong attachment to being right can be linked with a decreased capacity for openness. This exercise will help you build awareness of how attached you are to being right.

Tick the box that corresponds with your level of agreement with each statement. Be honest with yourself. I also recommend checking your view against those of a few colleagues or family members who know you well enough to be honest with you.

1 = Strongly agree   4 = Disagree

2 = Agree   5 = Strongly disagree

3 = Neutral

	1	2	3	4	5
I am good at getting people round to my way of thinking					
People tend not to challenge me too much when it's clear I have set my mind on something					
I use logic to persuade people to my way of thinking					

	1	2	3	4	5
I get very irritated by people who say they agree with me, then keep asking questions					
I believe that once you've made your mind up about something, you should stick to that opinion					
I expect people to work as hard as I do					
I get very frustrated with people who promise to do something, then don't follow through					
I have very strong moral principles					
I struggle to work with people who don't share my morals					
If someone breaks my trust, I really struggle to work with them again					

As a guide, the more answers you have in the 'Agree' and 'Strongly agree' columns, the more likely you are to have a strong attachment to your view of the world being the right one. Don't judge yourself on whatever you have noted as being 'right' or 'wrong' in itself, because there is no right or wrong! With increased awareness of your natural tendencies you can make choices to being more open when necessary.

EXERCISE REVIEW

- What are your reflections on the ladder of inference?
- How can you use your ladder to help you stay open to seeing other versions of the truth?
- How could your ladder close you down from seeing other versions of the truth?
- As you completed the exercise, what examples came to mind of times when you haven't been open?

UNDERSTANDING YOUR BRAIN TO HELP YOU REMAIN OPEN

While the ladder of inference helps you understand that you see the world in a unique way, it's also useful to understand enough about how your brain functions so you can work with it to enhance your capability to be open.

We are hugely complex organisms and our brains have to work very hard to keep the human machine functioning. As a result, over millennia, our brains have found short-cuts to make our thought processes as efficient as possible, processing the millions of stimuli we receive every day through our five senses. There are many theoretical models that describe in huge amounts of detail our physiology and neurology. I find the following two models most useful when looking at the capacity to remain open.

Three-brain theory

The three-brain theory was proposed as a very simplified model of the brain in the 1960s by American physician and neuroscientist Paul D. MacLean[35]. While generally unpopular in the field of neuroscience, it is still hugely popular for lay people. Why is it still a useful reference point? Precisely due to its simplicity; the very thing that draws the criticism from the field. The model gives us enough of an approximation of what happens in our brain for us to enhance our understanding of what it is to be human, how we can change our relationship with our thoughts and what we can and can't control.

MacLean described the brain as having evolved in a hierarchy and in function as the human species evolved. His theory describes the following three areas of the brain.

---

35 MacLean, P. D. (1990) *The Triune Brain in Evolution: Role in Paleocerebral Functions*, Springer

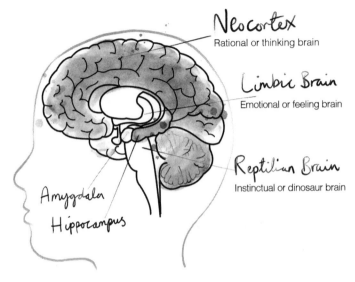

Neocortex
Rational or thinking brain

Limbic Brain
Emotional or feeling brain

Reptilian Brain
Instinctual or dinosaur brain

Amygdala

Hippocampus

Three-brain theory

1   Reptilian brain: approximately 500 million years old and the oldest part of our brain. It controls the body's vital functions such as heart rate, breathing, body temperature and balance. It includes the main structures found in a reptile's brain that are responsible for instinctual behaviours involved in aggression, dominance, territoriality, and ritual displays. The reptilian brain is reliable but tends to be somewhat rigid and compulsive. You may also recognise this description from the bestselling *Chimp Paradox*[36] by Professor Steve Peters of Sky ProCycling fame.

2   Limbic system: approximately 200 million years old, having emerged in the very first mammals. It records memories of behaviours that produced agreeable and disagreeable

36 Peters, S. (2012) *The Chimp Paradox: The Mind Management Programme to Help You Achieve Success, Confidence and Happiness*, Vermilion

experiences and uses those memories to create emotions. The main structures of the limbic brain are the hippocampus, the amygdala and the hypothalamus. The limbic brain is the seat of the value judgements that we make that exert such a strong influence on our behaviour (think back to the ladder of inference). It's also the part of the brain that fires the fight or flight response described earlier.

3   Neocortex: the youngest part of our brain is approximately 3.5 million years old. This part was first found in primates and evolved to encompass what modern neuroscience understands as many different layers. You are likely to have heard of the different types of cortex (visual, auditory and motor) and the different lobes of the brain contained within the neocortex. However, to keep to the simplicity of MacLean's model, the neocortex is responsible for functions such as human language, abstract thought, spatial reasoning, imagination, consciousness and generation of motor commands. The neocortex is flexible and has almost infinite learning capabilities.

System 1 and system 2 thinking

Daniel Kahneman is an Israeli-American psychologist notable for his work on the psychology of judgement and decision making, as well as behavioural economics. He was awarded the 2002 Nobel Memorial Prize in Economic Sciences. I read his book *Thinking, Fast and Slow*[37] when it was published in 2011. It was a bit of a heavy read, but the research findings, theories and applications of his work were an epiphany for me, building on what I already knew about how our brains work.

---

37 Kahneman, D. (2012) *Thinking, Fast and Slow*, Penguin

The key element of Kahneman's book that is relevant for developing your skill in being open, is the acceptance that you may not think as carefully and logically as you believe. Look back at the first exercise in this chapter on page 102, where you looked at the strength of your belief in your world view. Some of the questions looked at how much you pushed your viewpoint. If you are anything like me, you're more likely to push something when you feel like you've given it a lot of thought, rationally examined all the facts and made the best decision for the way forward. And here's the shocker – Kahneman proved that, in reality, your brain rarely thinks carefully and rationally. The type of thinking that we believe we apply to our most complex problems is effortful, logical, calculating and conscious; Kahneman calls this 'slow thinking or system 2'. He differentiates this with 'fast thinking or system 1', which is automatic, frequent, emotional, stereotypic and unconscious (think back to the ladder of inference). We believe we use system 2 (slow) thinking for our greatest challenges, but our brains are inherently lazy and look for the path of least effort.

To illustrate this, answer the following:

> *A bat and a ball cost $1.10. The bat costs $1 more than the ball. How much does the ball cost?*
>
> *Answer: _____*

This question is one of three devised by Professor Shane Frederick from Yale School of Management to test how easily students can switch off their initial reaction and answer (system 1) in favour of a more considered and thought through answer (system 2).

Approximately 80% of the people reading this book will have answered ten cents. If that was your answer, I can tell you now that your brain has taken the easy road to get to that answer – system 1 thinking – and that you are wrong! Knowing that, now see what it feels like to try and use your system 2 thinking. Look at the question again to get to the correct answer. When I first came across this question I found getting to the right answer difficult and hugely frustrating. The correct answer is five cents. Oh, and if you got it right first time, this doesn't mean you are immune to system 1 thinking, it just means you may have a different relationship to maths problem solving! Please read on.

You can now feel how system 2 (slow) thinking requires significantly more effort than system 1 (fast) thinking and see that your brain will use the easiest combination of the two systems to reach a decision or perform an action. There's another twist – over time, a task that needs initially to be performed by system 2 will eventually get transferred to system 1 as you get used to it. Once transferred, you rely on the 'lazy' system 1 thinking, and this is when you can be prone to make mistakes as you stop the deliberate, logical, calculating thinking of system 2.

Kahneman's body of work and the theories in his book are much deeper and wider than the system 1 and system 2 briefly discussed here. His thinking has also been taken forward by many eminent scientists and psychologists. A recent publication on the subject is by David Robson, ex *New Scientist* and BBC Future editor specialising in topics relating to neuroscience and psychology. His book *The Intelligence Trap*[38] combines research, case studies and stories to demonstrate that smart people are just as prone to making mistakes as everyone else. In fact, they may be even *more* susceptible to making mistakes!

My goal in bringing this body of work into your awareness is to highlight the illusion of clear thinking. Accepting that you are not as strategic and thoughtful as you might believe is another challenge to the strength of attachment you have to your world view, and to that view being right. Remember, the overall purpose of this chapter is to encourage greater openness.

---

38 Robson, D. (2019) *The Intelligence Trap*, Hodder & Stoughton

PSYCHOLOGICAL TRIGGERS

Chapter 2 explored the fight or flight response and how it affects our bodies. The extra layer of information I'd like to add here is the extraordinary effect the fight or flight response has on your cognitive function. When you are triggered into that response, your brain temporarily loses the ability to connect with your neocortex. When this happens you are physiologically incapable of logical thought. Thus, your cognitive function is impaired and you may do something in the moment that is completely outside the realm of normality for you. That action may in turn create additional triggers, thereby sustaining the fight or flight response for even longer. It's a destructive vicious circle.

There are more and more social media clips shaming people for appalling triggered behaviour. The situations often seem insignificant (for example, an uncomfortable seat on a long haul flight, a driving incident) but for the people who experience the loss of control it's all about their own ladder of inference and what's created that trigger.

You might be understanding this at an academic/rational level, but try to recall a specific time when your response to something went over the top. Look at that event and your behaviour in the context of having lost your capability for rational thought in that moment. It's not an excuse for bad behaviour, but I find knowing that there is a physiological reason for temporary loss of control is fascinating. Your responsibility is to increase awareness of what your triggers are; to be able to notice them and take action to take your body out of the fight or flight response and reduce the amount of time your brain is hijacked. This will help you avoid behaviour you'll later regret.

In psychology, the term 'trigger' is often associated with trauma, whereby a stimulus prompts recall of a previous traumatic experience. The stimulus itself need not be frightening nor traumatic and could be only indirectly or superficially reminiscent of an earlier traumatic incident (for example, a smell or a sound). Even so, that stimulus can trigger a full fight or flight response. The purpose of thinking about triggers in this chapter is to help you identify things that shut down your capability to be open. The triggers may not be on the scale of a previous trauma, but they are things that cause you significant irritation, and to which you have a very swift fight or flight response (for example, heart rate increase, breathing faster, a strong feeling of frustration or anger).

Getting to know your triggers

It can be very difficult to stop ourselves being triggered as it's such a hard-wired response. So, the work is less about trying to stop the trigger, and more about building your awareness of what triggers you. With increased awareness you can develop your ability to choose how you respond. This exercise will help you build that awareness.

Complete the grid on the worksheet on the next page.

Description of trigger	Strength of trigger (1 = weak; 10 = strong)	What feelings do I experience?	

- Column 1: make a list of the things that irritate you. Think broadly: other people's behaviour; specific words; things people wear; politics or beliefs; environmental factors; certain noises, smells, etc.
- Column 2: consider the strength of each trigger on a scale of 1–10.
- Column 3: what feelings does each trigger bring up in you?
- Column 4: think about how you change when you are triggered.
- Column 5: how do people experience you when each trigger occurs? For example, do you get up, stomp around and/or wave your arms around? Does your voice get louder/harsher? Do you verbally attack? Do you sulk or go silent? Does your face go red?
- Column 6: think about the impact of your triggered response on others. Are you shutting down conversations through your reactions? Is your triggered response creating a trigger in the other person?

Finally, ask some of your support team to carry out the same exercise (don't share your grid with them first).

	What behaviours do I adopt in response?	Describe how people experience me when I am triggered by this	Negative impact of trigger on others (1 = low impact; 10 = high impact)

EXERCISE REVIEW

- What did you notice about your emotions as you completed the table?
- How open were you to hearing what your support team offered in response to this exercise?
- If your inner voice was discounting some views as 'wrong', what can you learn from this?
- What else did you notice when using the worksheet as a diary?

You might also find it useful to use the same worksheet as a live document to record what happens over the next week or two. This would further enhance your self-awareness.

TAKING RESPONSIBILITY FOR YOUR TRIGGERED REACTIONS

When you are triggered and react to situations in ways you wish you hadn't, it can be tempting to pass blame for your bad behaviour. You can 'blame' another person, something they said, the way they said it, the situation, the politics, the weather… you get the drift; anything to divert attention away from the fact that the bad behaviour is yours and yours alone.

The bottom line is only you are responsible for the way you act. No one else has control over that.

From the previous exercise, you're starting to get to know your triggers. So once triggered, how can you get yourself back to your 'untriggered' state? Here are two simple steps to get the access to your neocortex back again:

1 Notice when you've been triggered

This isn't always easy, but the more you practise this the earlier you'll notice when you're triggered. When first working with this, many of my clients report only noticing they've been triggered after it was too late (for example, they've said something they wish they hadn't).

> One business owner I worked with was aware that he got triggered when his Board didn't offer enough challenge. His frustration would grow to the point that he would slam his fist on the table and shout, 'I wish you would all challenge me more!' He soon realised that he was in a vicious cycle where his behaviour was shutting down their willingness to challenge – the very opposite of what he wanted. During our work together, he started to notice where his trigger began and, over time, identified

its first sign as being a tension in the little finger of his right hand. With that knowledge he could then take some of the other steps outlined below to take control of himself. This meant he avoided getting to the fully triggered state where he shouted and slammed his fist on the table. Brilliantly, this client also developed the capability to be open with his colleagues once he'd made the connection between his own behaviour and shutting them down. He became open enough to see his own behaviour for what it was, together with being open with his team, talking to them about his new awareness and insight. This combination set the Board on the path to more constructive meetings.

2 Choose your response(s)

Based on the strength of the trigger, choose from the options below:

- Create time out (for when it's a strong trigger): give yourself space away from the situation (for example, go to the bathroom, go and make a coffee) then use the other techniques below.

- Focus on your breathing: be conscious of your posture, pull your shoulders down and back and shift your breath from your upper chest to your abdomen. Abdominal breathing (where you focus on filling up the lower part of your lungs just above your belly button) triggers the vagus nerve, which will activate your parasympathetic nervous system and regulate your body back to normal and away from its triggered state.

- Choose one or two of the following five senses and focus:
  - See: notice something in the room and focus on it.
  - Hear: listen for sounds to distract you.
  - Smell: notice aromas around you, or smell something you like (for example, an essential oil).
  - Taste: generally best to avoid food for stress relief (as we discussed in Chapter 2).
  - Touch: focus on where your body is connecting with a chair, or where your feet connect with the ground.

Whichever sense you choose, hold the focus for as long as you can, and keep coming back to it when you get distracted.

WHAT ELSE CAN YOUR TRIGGERS TELL YOU?

Your brain is so clever that it supresses memories of when you act in ways that are contradictory to your beliefs (which we all do from time to time). When you see someone else operating in that contradictory way your reptilian brain goes into high gear and you become hyper-alert and sensitive. A useful short-hand for this theory was recently coined by Harvard University graduate Dr Martha Beck – she called it 'You spot it, you got it'. In other words, you are triggered by anything that reminds you of the behaviour you're denying in yourself.

> *'Everything that irritates us about others can lead us to an understanding of ourselves.'*
>
> **Carl Jung**

Over 10 years ago, I remember feeling complete outrage when a therapist offered this theory up to me. She suggested that the behaviour I was railing against in a colleague might be something I also did from time to time. I was genuinely furious. It took me many months to accept the solid psychological research behind this theory. Having accepted it, I was able to see this 'blind-side' element to some triggers and soften my response to those things, and the people who were triggering me. It's been a hugely helpful model to call to mind over the years.

Adapting your triggered response

This exercise will help you choose which triggers to really get to know and work on, so you can adapt your response.

Look back at your grid, and your support team's grid, from the 'getting to know your triggers' exercise on page 111.

1   **a)** Which triggers had the highest negative impact on others?

b) For these triggers, consider your strategies for managing your reactions.

2   Now, look at your list of triggers (and those offered by your support team) and consider them in light of the 'You spot it, you got it' theory. You are human, so there will be at least one trigger in your list that is a behaviour you exhibit but don't like to acknowledge! Make notes on your thoughts.

Working with your triggers is hard. You are trying to undo a hard-wired response that is linked to your ladder of inference. It is important work, though. Sometimes you'll be able to notice the trigger and control your response, sometimes you won't. Even with all the knowledge I have about these various models there are still times when I am unable to spot a trigger.

I remember one occasion a few years ago when I had put a lot of effort into organising a weekend away for a friend's significant birthday. I had spent time on the arrangements and had requested that members of the group bring different foods, drinks, etc. They had all agreed. I sent a final confirmation email four days ahead of the weekend, reminding everyone of the details. As everyone arrived I checked that they'd brought what they had agreed. One friend said, 'No, I didn't bring that, it wasn't on my list.' Her response triggered me. I couldn't recognise my trigger quickly enough to stop me snapping at her that it 'definitely *was* on your list'. After that I had two options: either talk to her about how we could go about getting the ingredient; or dig out the emails to prove the ingredient was on the list. But my snappy response had, in turn, triggered her, so she wasn't interested in the email proof I offered her. She didn't apologise; just shrugged her shoulders and said, 'Oh, I must have missed that' and walked off. I remained triggered for quite a long time. If I had been able to access my neocortex, I would have chosen to have a conversation about how we went about getting the missing ingredient, which I am sure she would have helped with. As it panned out, my response shut her down and I grudgingly went to the supermarket (a 30-minute roundtrip) myself. Only on that drive was I able to reflect, be open and see what had happened for what it was. I could see that this situation pulled on two of my triggers:

- People not doing what they say they will.
- People not fully reading emails that I've spent ages compiling (which I also know is a 'You spot it, you got it' scenario. I skim-read things, too).

My reflection on that drive (and the space away from the situation) allowed me to calm down. On my return, I apologised to her for snapping, after which she apologised for having missed the ingredient. We both wanted to create a lovely experience for our friend's birthday, so we were able to focus on that (and the weekend was fantastic).

REFLECTION

Before moving on to Chapter 4, and in addition to the outputs from your exercises, make notes on the following:

Things that surprised me in this chapter:

Things I found most useful in this chapter:

Things I'm not so sure about/are sceptical about:

If you have noted anything directly above, see if you can consider what you now know about how your brain operates to identify where that scepticism is coming from.

Other thoughts that are bubbling around in my mind:

CHAPTER 4

Insight

INTRODUCTION

In the last chapter we looked at tools and techniques to help you be more open and connect with yourself at a deeper level. As a result, you are likely to have a number of things bubbling around in your mind. Using the exercises in this book, you've started to increase your self-awareness and you may be starting to see your habits and behaviours in a different light. The focus of this chapter is to help you work with the thoughts that have arisen so far, and help you focus on those that have the potential to be an insight, rather than just be thoughts that are interesting. In her Radio 4 podcast 'Epiphanies'[39], writer and academic A. L. Kennedy describes an insight as being 'a message that has such an impact it almost asks to be acted on'.

According to Marshall Goldsmith in his book *What Got You Here Won't Get You There*, the strategies that have got you to this point in your life may no longer be the most relevant to help you achieve the future you want[40]. This chapter will help you zone in on the areas you may need to shift to enable your future success. People often refer to an insight as an 'aha moment'. In the aforementioned Radio 4 podcast, Neuroscientist Daniel Glaser describes how these aha moments often 'feel like they are coming from outside our heads' but goes on to explain that 'they actually come from outside our knowledge of what's going on in our heads... it's a sudden noticing of the work we've been doing in our heads (but may not have been aware of)'. Each chapter and the exercises in this book so far will have got your subconscious going – so you are in a good place to start coaxing your insights.

---

39 https://www.bbc.co.uk/programmes/b09ycvts
40 Goldsmith, M. (2008) *What Got You Here Won't Get You There*, Profile Books

COAXING INSIGHTS

The thing about arriving at an insight is that you can't just set aside time in your diary to have one; hence the popular saying 'I do my best thinking in the shower/bath/walking'. You may well know this in principle, but your driven nature means you can be impatient for things to happen. I

'An insight is a bit like a cat, it can be coaxed but it won't usually come when called.'
Carola Salvi

find the following description of an insight by cognitive neuroscientist Carola Salvi really useful in helping me to resist the impatience when I feel it building.

So far, the exercises in this book have all been geared towards enabling you to reflect on things in different ways. The notes you have made at the end of each chapter are where we will pick up now. There are three territories here that will help you get into the zone where insights may appear.

1 Hang out with your thoughts

As a driven person you are likely to be pretty quick to act and move forward, and you may pay less attention to your thoughts than you do to your actions. You are also less likely to dwell on things and reflect on them after they have happened. This natural tendency can make it even harder to create the space for insights to arrive. So thinking of your thoughts as that cat may help. Hang out with them, notice them, be inquisitive about them, then let them go again before coming back to them a while later. See what happens.

You may get a strong sense of which thoughts are insights that demand to be acted on, you may only get a vague feeling. The important thing here is not to fall back into a previous mindset trying to know what is right or wrong… you can't know right from wrong here. If you are judging your thoughts using your ladder of inference only, your future will only be dictated by your past.

Rachel and I had been working together over a period of six months and were having our third coaching session. In the first two sessions, she had been frustrated by what she saw as her colleagues' lack of motivation and drive to achieve the business targets she was setting. I could hear the energy in her voice when she talked not only about her work, but also about her exercise and fitness training for a gruelling mountain running race. As she told that story, she also started to express disbelief that in the evening all her colleagues did was socialise with friends. Her judgement was that they didn't have any 'get up and go' outside of work. As I asked her questions, her awareness grew. She realised she was expecting everyone to be like her; in her opinion, her way of living was the only way to get the most out of life. She left that phone call with increased awareness, but there was no insight at that point. We diarised our next phone call for eight weeks later.

The next session came around and Rachel told me about how she'd been thinking about the awareness raised in our last conversation and that she'd been aware how strongly she'd been judging her colleagues. Her awareness also extended to friends and family and she described how she'd had this uncomfortable feeling bubbling around. She told me she'd been thinking a lot *about what she'd said during the previous call. About three weeks later, Rachel recounted how she had burst into tears while driving to the Welsh mountains to go fell-running. She had such a strong emotional experience she had to pull the car over and stop. She spoke with huge speed and urgency about how she'd realised her judgement itself was actually making her team less motivated and how, in that moment, in tears in the lay-by, she realised she needed to change her mindset and how she interacted with her team. She took action the next day and apologised to her team, explaining the revelation she'd been through. In the three weeks between then and our phone call, she had noticed significant improvement in the mood of the team and, as a consequence, the success they were experiencing.*

Rachel's story is a cracking example of how different awareness and insight are. Awareness we can sit with, insight demands action. Rachel's story also shows how insights take time to emerge. Rachel's hit her like a ton of bricks. They don't all hit you that strongly, but the biggest insights that have the potential for the biggest change often do – so don't resist any surges of emotion as you go through this book, embrace them for what they could bring.

2 Get to know your inner voice

Your inner voice can either kill your insights before they are fully formed or enable them to flourish. You won't be able to silence your inner critic, but you may be able to change your relationship with them.

If there is an awareness of something or thought that's bubbling into an insight, your inner voice may try and pull you away from it. If we go back to Rachel's example, she told me how she'd been grappling with that uncomfortable awareness of judgement, but that her inner voice kept telling her she was right. Until she let go of that (probably subconsciously, as on that drive she was focused on the act of driving itself) she couldn't allow that insight to land.

If you're struggling to hear your inner voice, try listening to, or watching, a podcast/programme where something is being debated. As you listen or watch you will have an internal commentary on what you are hearing: 'I wouldn't have done that', 'That's a crazy thing to say', 'I know that's wrong', etc. That is your inner voice talking. Your inner voice is always there, sometimes it's a cheerleader, sometimes it's a coach, other times it's a defeatist or naysayer.

The trick is to be able to choose your relationship with what you hear your inner voice saying. Until we become aware of the voice, there is a temptation to just accept what it is saying. However, if you think of it as a good friend whose advice or commentary you can choose to take or not, you can soften its capacity to limit your thinking and actions.

The voices of your cheerleader and naysayer may have different qualities to them. Some of my clients find it useful to identify differences in gender, tone, pitch and volume of their positive and negative inner voices, and some even like to give each of them a name – but I'll leave that up to you. The objective is for you to do whatever you need to do to be able to tune into the voice(s).

In relation to the work you're doing in this book, you'll have the same internal narrative running alongside your thoughts, and in many exercises you'll have explicitly tuned into what that inner voice might be saying. When it comes to insights, it's even more important to pay attention to when this inner voice might be preventing the breakthrough to an epiphany.

3 Choose your method to capture your thinking

Everyone has different preferences in how they capture information. You may be a list person, a spreadsheet person, a pen and paper person, a person who likes to use visuals and colour on paper. Alternatively, you may not feel compelled to capture anything at all. There are a number of research findings over recent years that point to the pen being mightier than the laptop to help cognitive processing of information[41]. Whatever your natural pre-disposition, I encourage you to capture your thoughts from this chapter using pen on paper. In addition, to help keep the brain open (rather than fall into linear process thinking that tends to happen with lists or spreadsheets), I would recommend using a mind-mapping technique with colour and/or symbols (for example, happy, sad, angry faces, ticks and crosses) to capture your thinking as it emerges. However, all the above said, this is your choice – so work with what feels best for you.

---

41 Mueller, P. A. and Oppenheimer, D. M. (2014) 'The Pen Is Mightier Than the Keyboard: Advantages of Longhand Over Laptop Note Taking', *Psychological Science*

WHAT DOES AN INSIGHT LOOK LIKE?

I describe a deep insight as having the following components:

1 An awareness of a thought or behaviour that is showing up in the here and now that is having an impact you don't like.

2 An awareness of that same thought or behaviour being present in a number of situations in your past.

3 An appreciation for how that thought or behaviour might have served you well in the past.

4 An understanding that in your current situation the impact of the thought or behaviour isn't serving you well.

5 An awareness that if you managed to change your relationship with the thought, or shift your behaviour the outcome and/or impact is likely to be improved.

Point 3 above is key. Insights are not about beating yourself up for whatever you've been doing to this point in your life. Have compassion for that old version of you and what you did to get where you are now. The purpose of insights is to help you move forward in the direction you now choose.

Here are some examples of key insights that have evolved for me over the years, just to give you a sense of how varied they can be. These insights combine to help me make choices. Some big choices you've already read about, but there are also little choices I make every day. (For example, do I make myself go to the gym or do I take a gentle walk?) Some of the insights were a joy to discover – giving me a real sense of freedom. Some were deeply challenging – to the point where I rejected them completely, but they came back to me years later in ways that couldn't be ignored.

A tendency to take responsibility for things outside my control.

As with many insights, we can usually follow things quite a long way back into our past if we want to. If I think about my work life, I always took on responsibility: pitches no one thought we could win; delivering leading edge solutions when my Board-level peers weren't sure we could; speaking up when others wouldn't.

In my family I'm the oldest of my siblings. I have two younger brothers (two and four years younger than me). As a child, my parents regularly used the 'you are the oldest, set an example' line to get me to behave, and that led me to feel a great sense of responsibility. There's one particular photo of me holding one of my brothers by his hands as he teetered on his two chubby little legs; my parents used to look at the picture and say, 'That's when you taught Irving to walk'. For most of my childhood I truly believed I had taught my brother to walk; what a thing to have achieved!

As I moved into adulthood, the responsibility thing continued to manifest itself. It wasn't until after I'd decided to leave my husband that I realised my sense of responsibility had got out of hand. I had felt responsible for my husband's life. For 10 years of our marriage he spent around six months a year in a deep depression accompanied by suicidal thoughts. He repeatedly told me that if it wasn't for me, he'd be dead. He told me if I ever left him, he would kill himself. He refused counselling or started (probably to please me) then stopped. I took all that on because I believed I could help him. He was never sectioned as I was doing such a great job of caring for him. I look back on some of the therapy conversations I had when I was married and can hear the questions I was asked in a different light now. Questions such as 'Do you think it's reasonable to feel responsible for someone else's life?', 'Do you think it's normal to feel responsible for your husband flying into a rage and breaking x, y and z (always inanimate objects)?' At the time, I didn't let these questions fully land with me. I deflected them with great skill. Changing my relationship with responsibility was one of my most fundamental insights, which led to the most difficult decision I have ever made – to leave the marriage knowing and accepting that my husband may take his own life as a result. I had to work really hard to be able to see that whatever he did was his responsibility *not* mine.

Thinking rather than feeling.

My natural preference is thinking rather than feeling. I've always known this and once, in the corporate world, this was confirmed by psychometric tests like MBTI®, DiSC® and Insights®. I also knew that those tools are underpinned by the personality types and functions described by Carl Jung. I fully identified with the descriptions and saw thinking over feeling as a massive strength. However, I didn't pay attention to what that preference could do in overdrive – i.e. not letting me notice when what I was experiencing was potentially bad for my health and wellbeing. When I started having counselling after my breakdown I remember my counsellor asking, 'How do you feel about that?' She asked that specific question a lot. I used to answer and we'd move on. In the third session, as I started to answer yet another 'How do you feel about that?' question, she gently stopped me half way through. 'Janine, can I interrupt? I notice that when you answer questions about how you feel, you don't answer how you feel. I notice you always tell me what you think. I'd really like you to try and answer with how you feel.' It floored me. I really couldn't get there. I'd lost the ability to feel. My experiences over the years had been so challenging I'd shut my emotions off and stayed in thinking mode. It took a long time to rediscover not only how to connect with feeling, but also to find the language to describe it.

A distorted relationship with the notion of control.
Our human nature is to want to make sense of things. When things around us are out of control, we seek to control what we can.

During my marriage, because my husband's illness was totally out of control I focused on my work, probably over-controlling the poor colleagues I worked with a lot of the time. I had hoped my divorce would give me my life back. But five months afterwards, everything was falling away around me. My father had secondary cancer in his bones and was deteriorating; my mother had a serious heart condition and needed urgent bypass surgery; and we'd merged two businesses together and as part of a Board restructure I was given notice of redundancy. This was a complete shock. I felt abandoned by a company I'd worked with for over 10 years and had given blood, sweat and tears to in pursuit of success.

So in that year of chaos, my 14-year marriage having collapsed and my relationship with my long-term employer potentially also coming to an abrupt end, I did what author, leader and educator Dr Anthony Kasozi[42] found to be true; when faced with upheaval we seek to control what we can. Thus, I controlled the things I could. For me, that was what I ate and how I exercised. I exercised intensely, and I focused

---

42 http://anthonykasozi.info/

obsessively on eating healthily (all of which I discussed in Chapter 2). My insight around this didn't come until that Kaliyoga retreat in Spain; a full five years after my breakdown.

Only seeing my drive for work as a positive.

I never ever considered that my drive to succeed could be anything other than positive. However, I came to realise that it could have unintended consequences not only for me, but also for my team. Like Rachel's example earlier on page 125, my expectation of others was that they should be as driven as me, and I struggled to understand if they weren't. I became aware that I was good at listening to people, but not great at taking account of what I'd heard in how I then pushed things forward. I had a tendency to ignore or minimise people's concerns in my drive for the end goal. I ignored their concerns in the same way I ignored my own body trying to tell me it, too, was concerned. To this day, I hold this insight and my awareness of my drive at the very front of my mind. It's something I regularly have to check myself on. My partner and my coach are the two main members of my support team who help me notice (if I haven't noticed myself) when I slip back into overdrive and take too much on.

My needs are as important as everyone else's

My compassion and my drive were a toxic combination. My work and my husband came before my own wellbeing. You read in the Prologue how that was playing out. I was spectacularly brilliant at not paying attention to what I needed to be healthy and, yet, through all that, I managed to be a high performer at work. If you looked at external measures such as promotions, bonuses and pay rises, I was highly successful. Getting to this insight was painfully hard work. I eventually accepted that my needs were equal to everyone else's and sometimes (shock horror) it was even OK to prioritise my needs over others'. It's another one of the insights I have to continually remind myself of to prevent me not slipping into old habits.

Listening to my body.

People have said 'listen to your body' to me hundreds and hundreds of times over the years. Over 20 years ago I had a close Australian friend who was a massage therapist and way ahead of her time in what she practised. She used to give me a really hard time for not being in tune with my body. Intellectually I understood what was being said, but on the rare occasions when I actually noticed things weren't right, I looked externally for reasons and wanted a quick diagnosis and fix. My version of listening to my body was to book myself into a health spa for a few days when I felt at my wits end. But instead of relaxing, I'd then book myself into every exercise class going.

These insights are now part of me. They offer me new and different lenses through which to see the world. Lenses that I find useful and that I know will support me in whatever future I wish to create. It's also worth noting that these insights can remain uncomfortable and confronting when they reappear in different guises, long after you think you've got a handle on them.

Coaxing your insights

I hesitated to provide an exercise in this chapter as coaxing insights is fluid and occurs over a period of time. So this is less of an exercise per se, and more of a set of questions that may be useful for you as you let your insights develop.

Please don't use the bullets as a linear process to work through. Read all the bullet points first and then decide what feels right for you in how to sit with your thoughts over time, using whatever capture method you have chosen.

- Re-read your final reflection notes from the end of each chapter. You may have written these a while ago now, so notice any immediate reactions that come up for you when re-reading your own thoughts.
- Let whatever is coming up sit with you for a while (this could be a few days or a few weeks or even longer).
- Pay attention to your feelings and the narrative of your inner voice – noticing if they change over time.
- Pay particular attention to thoughts that elicit feelings of being unsure/uncomfortable, but at the same time somewhat exciting. What's your inner voice saying about those particular thoughts?
- Where thoughts are bringing up strong negative emotions or scepticism, think back to the 'You spot it, you got it' theory – what are you hiding from yourself?
- Which thoughts support the shifts you considered important back in Chapter 1? Which thoughts are strongly in the territory of helpers from Chapter 2?
- What thoughts are you strongly resisting? What needs to happen for you to be receptive to these thoughts?

I haven't defined the output of this exercise, as you will have chosen your own method of capture.

REFLECTION

This template is a way of consolidating your thinking in this chapter after having coaxed your insights over whatever period of time feels right for you, using whatever capture method feels appropriate. As a practice, this openness, self-reflection and insight coaxing is one that I encourage you to build into your life from this point forward. I recommend it's something you come back to again and again.

My emerging insights:

Insights that are bubbling, but I'm not quite ready to embrace yet:

What I have noticed about how I responded to this chapter:

My insights that are demanding action right now are the following (NB: I recommend capturing these using your choice of capture method discussed above):

CHAPTER 5

INTRODUCTION

As you move through the Choices™ programme, it's important to be kind to yourself and recognise the energy that this kind of work takes. You may have been surprised at how tired you felt after completing some of the exercises. Much of that will be due to you using a lot of your system 2 (slow) thinking, which is more physiologically taxing. Working on our own mindset, emotions and behaviour is hard work. In this chapter, my goal is to give you some information and frameworks that will help you stay with the programme, as well as strategies to help you deal with times when you are stuck.

GET COMFORTABLE WITH THE UNKNOWN

Many driven, successful people manage to create a lot of certainty in their lives. This is partly created by goal setting and having a clear sense of purpose. Life in our modern world is however far from certain. An old military acronym, VUCA, is now widely used in strategic leadership and development. VUCA stands for volatile, uncertain, complex and ambiguous.

- **Volatile**: the rate of change is increasing all the time. There really is no such thing as the status quo any more. Back in my corporate days, we used to talk about a 'new normal' or BAU (business as usual) after a business transformation had been completed. But there is no normal any more or, more accurately, constant change is now normal.
- **Uncertain**: in a macro sense, there is increasing uncertainty about the future, whether that be about politics, climate change or any number of things. In a micro sense, we are dealing with constant uncertainty in our lives and work, whether it be regarding the health of our close family and friends or the stability of our work.
- **Complex**: making decisions is getting more and more difficult due to multiple factors and the inter-relatedness of those factors on any decision. We can therefore feel stuck and not know how to move forward, as we can't predict the impact of those decisions.
- **Ambiguous**: even when something happens (think of recent significant political changes) there is less and less clarity about what that event will actually mean.

When you work on your inner motivations and feelings there can be a lot of not knowing. Being able to predict the actual outcome of any new approaches you decide to try is elusive:

'What would happen if I stopped looking at my emails over the weekend?'; 'What happens to my team if I don't make myself available to them all the time?' As you've seen in Chapter 4, your inner voice will have its own set of narratives on each insight you are working on. If you don't know for sure that a decision to act is the right one, it would be easy to feel unable to move forward. You stay stuck because you don't know what's right. But given we live in a VUCA world, how can you ever know if something is right?

Get used to accepting that you can't know. Get used to letting go of the need to know that something is right. All you can do is focus on the intent behind your chosen action or decision. If your intent is true to what you are trying to achieve, then the action is worth considering. Until you actually do something, you can't know for sure what the outcome will be.

> Sophie had a middle management role in the recruitment sector. She had been back from maternity leave for 12 months and was hugely frustrated as she didn't feel she was respected anymore. She felt that she was being passed over for opportunities to work on exciting projects that could have given her more profile and led to a potential promotion.
>
> Through our work together, Sophie came to the realisation that her inner voice was loud and constant: 'They don't respect me anymore.' This inner narrative became something she saw as fact. It wasn't. It was her own interpretation looking through her own ladder of inference. This 'fact' stopped her from asking to be involved in things, as she was fearful of rejection. Sophie retreated

into the dull work she knew well and could do standing on her head. She felt completely in control of that work but she didn't feel respected. She became completely stuck, watching other colleagues who she felt were less able than her do the higher profile work she wanted to do. This vicious cycle kept reinforcing her inner voice regarding her lack of respect.

A key insight for Sophie was that she realised she was afraid of the reaction if she spoke up. Sophie could suddenly see that her own actions were keeping her in a place she didn't want to be. She realised that if she did nothing different, things would stay the same. With these insights she could move herself into action. She spoke to her line manager, not to complain about what was wrong, but to request more involvement in different projects, which she placed in the context of wanting a future promotion. Within just a few weeks Sophie felt more motivated and energised by her work, which in turn helped her feel more respected.

Perspective check

This exercise will help you get yourself into action when the unknown and/or your inner voice has stopped you. This model is drawn from the work of Dr Chris Johnstone[43], an expert in the psychology of resilience. Using the physicality of the hand helps to get us out of our head (when our brains are overthinking things).

---

43 http://www.chrisjohnstone.info/

1   Pick an action that you feel you want to take, but (for whatever reason) find yourself unable to move forward with.

2   Now hold your hand out in front of you with your fingers splayed and make notes as you look at the hand. If I do x, y and z:

   a)   what's the worst that can happen? (lowest gap in your fingers)

   b)   what's the best that can happen? (highest gap in your fingers)

   c)   what's the most likely thing that will happen? (middle gap in your fingers)

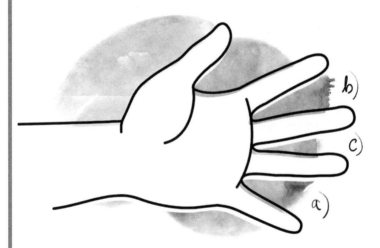

Perspective check

●   Notice how your brain probably found it easiest to think of the worst that could happen. Being drawn to this is why you are stuck.

- You may have scoffed at the ideas you came up with for c). Your internal naysayer voice may have shouted, 'That great stuff is never going to happen!' This is normal, when you are focused on the worst; you are a long way from believing that the best outcome is possible. However, the simple act of articulating a best outcome helps you to shift your thinking.

- Thus, when you got to looking at the most likely outcome, you probably had some hope that this was in fact possible. A shift away from the worst-case scenario, and a shift that should give you the impetus to do something, rather than accept the status quo.

Have this simple exercise in mind whenever you are facing something challenging and feel stuck.

UNDERSTAND AND USE YOUR ENERGY WISELY

As a driven person, you are more likely to find it hard to do nothing. Here's something to think about: as a driven person, your 'doing nothing' is someone else's doing something. On the occasions where I give myself permission for a whole day of doing nothing (more now than I used to, but still only two or three times a year) I find myself saying to someone about that day, 'I did absolutely nothing all day'. Even with all the work I've done to understand and manage my drive and nourish my success, saying that is still a small internal 'telling off'. What I am doing when I am doing nothing is more accurately described as doing something that I don't see as productive, and that I find very hard to do. Making cakes, doing crafts, going for walks, cleaning, reading… all of these feel productive. But sometimes I just need to switch off completely and watch some Netflix.

I could have let my thinking stop there, but a bit more reflection was useful to give me a deeper insight. In this example, my reflection led me back to the time when my brothers and I were between 8 and 15 years old. My dad strongly encouraged us not to turn the television on when we got home from school unless we had already chosen what we were going to watch. He called switching on the TV just to see what was on 'indiscriminate viewing'. I'll never forget that phrase. It sounded so grand and like something that was definitely bad for you. Then, when I was 15, the first breakfast TV show was launched. His attention turned to that, and we weren't allowed to have the TV on in the morning; if we had some spare time, we had to do something 'educational' before school. My mother (the ex-Olympic ice skater and a formidable woman) never stopped either; with three children and a household to run she had numerous small business enterprises over the years and would always be busy in the kitchen. I can't think of a single occasion when I saw my mother 'rest'. I can see how that early framing of the need to be focused and productive has shaped my drive, and there are many more examples. I look back with affection on my childhood influences, but can also now see that I need to take my foot off the 'drive' pedal sometimes to renew my energy.

We are all different, and different activities energise and deplete us. The psychometric tests that are based on Carl Jung's personality types look at this; tests such as Insights, DiSC, MBTI, ICS Connect. If you have ever completed one of these, dig them out to re-familiarise yourself with what energises you. If you haven't completed one, you'll be able to find a local practitioner in these tools to work with. According to Jung (diagram on next page), we all have personality types that exist on a spectrum of introversion to extraversion and thinking to feeling. In case you wondered, I am top right: extroverted and thinking.

The important thing about considering what energises us is that it is not always related to what we are good at. For example, I am very good at detail if I put my mind to it, but I don't enjoy doing a spreadsheet for hours on end. I can sit still in a lecture for hours, but I'd much rather be doing something that was helping me learn in a more experiential way. I loved writing this book, but spending time on the detail of references and final checking with my editor wasn't as enjoyable as getting the words on the page as they flowed out of me.

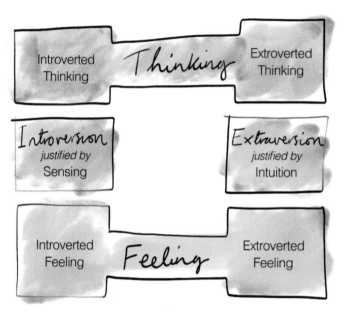

Personality types: based on the work of Carl Jung

It's also important to consider seasonality and how that affects your energy flows, and it will. If your inner voice is telling you that you have the same energy all year round, you're not listening to your body. During my Kaliyoga retreat I was really interested to hear the yoga teacher offer us this invitation: 'Recognise your body's natural response to the seasons, and don't expect the same of yourself throughout the year.' This was a bit of a revelation to me – one of those insights that appeared unexpectedly like that cat. I realised I used to beat myself up when I didn't have as much energy as I felt I should (especially in the winter months). I don't suffer from anything like Seasonal Affective Disorder, so I felt I should just push on through. The new insight allowed me to take action and develop a kinder self-narrative at the times of year when I don't feel as fully energised. I can now give myself permission and time to restore when my levels are low. This, in turn, means I hit my high-energy periods even more in my stride than before.

Personal energisers

This exercise is about looking at your life, your working life in particular, through a different lens (that of energisers) and using that awareness to make choices on how and when you use your energy.

This exercise has three parts. Use the worksheet to capture your responses.

Part 1: Can you identify your natural biorhythms? Your biorhythms are your personal cyclic pattern of physical, emotional and mental activity. If you are using a lot of caffeine and other stimulants that we looked at in Chapters 1 and 2, you may not be aware of your natural cycles, but see if you can identify them:

- When are you better at creative thinking versus detail?
- When do you find it easier to exercise?
- When are you in the right frame of mind for conversations you know may be challenging?
- Can you identify your high and low energy periods?

During the day:

- I generally feel most energised...
- I generally feel least energised...

During the week:

- I generally feel most energised...
- I generally feel least energised...

Do you have any times of the year when you feel less or more energised?

- I generally feel most energised in the following months of the year…
- I generally feel least energised in these months of the year…

Part 2: Use your understanding of your energy patterns to think differently about what you plan into your day. Think about your day-to-day work life and make a list of the full range of activities you get involved in. You might find it useful to group them and then think of the more detailed tasks within each group. For example, I think of my activities within the following blocks (detailed activities noted in brackets). I've listed these alphabetically. We're looking at how activities energise you here, not their importance.

- Admin (invoicing, expenses, management accounts, liaising with accountant)
- Client delivery (one-to-one coaching, workshops, speaking, training, not for profit work)
- Client prep work (designing workshops and Board away days, psychometric test set-ups, etc.)
- Health and wellbeing (activity built into my day)
- Marketing – the doing not the planning (social media posts, website management)
- Networking (attending industry functions) and new business meetings (meeting prospects)
- Personal development (attending training courses and webinars, reading, working with my supervisor)
- Strategy and business planning (of my own business)

- Travel
- Writing (blogs, book, opinion pieces)

Fill out the grid on your worksheet with your activities (either individually or in blocks) and make a note of how much they energise you on a scale of -5 to +5.

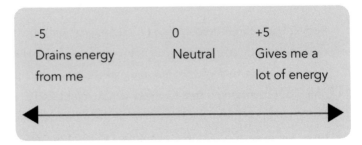

-5	0	+5
Drains energy from me	Neutral	Gives me a lot of energy

Activity	Energy score

Part 3: Now look back at your biorhythms (part 1 of this exercise) and think about your calendar and the times of day/week/year you are carrying out the activities.

Are there any changes you can make to ensure you are:

- harnessing your high-energy times and doing things that energise you further
- strategically choosing to do important but draining tasks when you are reasonably energised
- planning your time so you don't have full days of activities that drain you
- planning your time to inject energy boosters if you can't avoid long periods of draining activities.

What are the specific actions you will commit to making in how you manage your time?

One last thing to share with you on this... I go one step further in managing my time. I colour code my outlook calendar choosing different colours for task groups that energise me in different ways. I'm a very visual person, so with this I can easily see if I have a week where I have the potential to be out of balance. I can then think about actions that week that will give me an extra boost (or time to restore). This won't work for everyone but, if it appeals to you, give it a try.

Overall, I encourage you to think about your energy as something to manage and work with, not just something that's there to use up without thinking. Your energy is not finite, you need to recharge and renew it. This then links to the next topic, understanding your resilience.

UNDERSTAND YOUR OWN RESILIENCE

The word 'resilience' is being used more and more in the face of increasing levels of poor mental health in society. In a VUCA world, resilience is a vital quality that will contribute to our ability to cope.

Below are two definitions of resilience I choose to work with:

'Resilience is your ability to overcome, steer through and bounce back when adversity strikes.'

Karen Reivich and Andrew Shatté –

The Resilience Factor

'Resilience is the process of adapting well in the face of adversity or trauma, tragedy and even significant sources of stress.'

American Psychological Society

When I work with businesses to help people manage their stress and optimise their resilience, a starting assumption is that resilience is something you either have or don't have. I hear people say, 'She's really resilient' or describe themselves saying, 'I'm really resilient' or, conversely, 'I'm not very resilient'. If your internal narrative is that you are not resilient, you could just accept that as fact. If your internal narrative is that you are resilient, you can take it as a given that you will always be so. Prior to my breakdown, a big part of my self-identity was linked to being extremely resilient. I really valued what I saw as an inherent skill and assumed it would always be there. And, yet, life events happened and suddenly I found myself with no resilience at all. Terrifying on many levels.

So, when it comes to your resilience, have this narrative in your head: **My resilience is something I do, not just something I have.**

This thought makes it very clear that you can practise being resilient and get better at it, regardless of where you are starting from. If you see yourself as very resilient, the notion of taking care of that resilience may be new to you – but it's a crucial part of your toolkit to nourish your success.

Your resilience factors are completely personal to you; there is no judgement on what you need to do to stay resilient as no two people have the same tolerance for things. I can't stress this enough. What you need to do to remain resilient is yours and yours alone – don't feel tempted to compare yourself to

Sasha, a new business director, used to regularly attend pitch meetings with her MD. She used to admire his drive and commitment and would come to our coaching sessions and talk in awe of his ability to survive a hectic day simply drinking coffee, not eating anything and rarely even going to the bathroom. Sasha, being very driven, felt a need to mirror what she perceived as her successful MD's apparent resilience, but she found it difficult to maintain her own energy by matching what he did. In our work together, we explored what Sasha would be doing if she felt no judgement or pressure to be like someone else, but instead tuned into what she needed to thrive. She reached a deep insight that to take care of herself and maintain her energy she needed to drink less coffee and eat little and often – almost the opposite of what she had been doing.

others or allow yourself to feel judged or weak by needing to take time to restore.

My most powerful personal insight on the importance of managing my own resilience occurred on the day that it left me. I phoned our employee assistance programme and spoke to a counsellor. I was crying (those deep, chest-racking sobs), my breath was fast and shallow, I was shaking. It was like an out-of-body experience. Who was this person? I didn't know myself.

I remember rambling on about what was going on for me and how I should be able to cope but couldn't and how, 'This isn't like me, I don't understand what's going on'. I remember describing the feeling of standing on the edge of a cliff looking down and feeling like I was about to fall. The words 'I feel like I'm having a breakdown' tumbled out of my mouth...

I wanted the therapist to say, 'Of course you're not. You'll be fine. Here are a few exercises to do. You'll be back to normal in a few days'. He didn't. His response was, 'Yes, it sounds like you are'. I still feel a sense of nausea and vertigo remembering his words. All the reasons why I couldn't have a breakdown spilled out – 'busy... team need me... client not happy... mum and dad need me...' – the list went on. The counsellor listened patiently (probably having heard hundreds of executives in exactly the same position). He then offered me an analogy that has stayed with me ever since, and which I regularly use with my clients who are on the edge of overwhelm. Here it is:

Think about the last flight you took and cast your mind back to the safety demonstration. The cabin crew talk about the oxygen masks that will drop from the ceiling in the event of cabin pressure loss. Who do they tell you to put the mask on first? Adults or children? It's adults first. Why? Because if the adults lose consciousness, the children are not likely to able to fend for themselves.

And so it is for your own resilience and self-care. If you don't take care of yourself, you could get to the point where, for a period of time, you are not able to be of use to those you want to help/lead/nurture, etc.

Personal resilience factors

This exercise will help you identify the factors that increase or reduce your capacity to be resilient. You can make active choices to do things that will support your resilience, thereby nourishing your success.

Think of your resilience as a bucket[44].

- When the bucket is full of water, you are fully resourced, energised and resilient.
- When the water level is low, your resilience is less.
- When the bucket is empty you're in a bad place.

Using the worksheet, capture your thoughts.

What things fill up and keep the water level high in your bucket? Make a note of everything you can think of that energises you, allows you to renew your optimism, helps you to relax, feels

good for your soul. Look back at the wheel of focus exercise

---

44 Metaphor of a bucket in this context borrowed from fellow leadership specialist Heather Wright. www.advance-performance.co.uk

from Chapter 1 on page 19 for inspiration if you need to, and/or ask people from your support team what they think would keep your water level high. Review the helpers you identified from Chapter 2 also.

What things make dents and holes in your bucket that allow the water to leak out? Make a note of everything that saps your energy. Think about whether each thing is a dent or a hole (and how big that hole might be). Many of these will be the opposites of what  you've noted above, but there are likely to be additional things to make note of (look back at the 'getting to know your triggers' exercise in Chapter 3 on page 111).

Thinking about the dents in your bucket is useful as you may ignore the cumulative effect of things that reduce your resilience. A repeated dent in the same place will eventually become a hole. Thinking of the holes as various sizes is also useful. Large holes (resilience zappers) are generally more noticeable and you may pay attention when they happen, but when you're in the middle of something really important that you're driven to achieve, you may be ignoring the smaller holes. You may be able to manage with one reasonably small hole in your resilience bucket if you can top the water up enough, but add lots of small holes (which you may consider as insignificant things) and the water may flow out too quickly for you to maintain the level, even if you top it up.

You now have a better understanding of your resilience factors. These will shift and change as you move through life, so keep in touch with what you need to ensure that water level remains high. My clients often come to me feeling very over-stressed and will blame their employer, their work or someone else for the holes in their bucket. I used to do the same. But no one else can manage your resilience for you. Only you know what you need. I encourage you to take responsibility for the water level in your bucket.

WHAT CAN YOU ACTUALLY CONTROL?

You looked at your capability to be open in Chapter 3. If your starting point was to be pretty attached to your version of the truth being the right one, you are more likely to retreat into that behaviour when you are under pressure. However, even if you are naturally quite open to other versions of the truth, as a human, you have an in-built need to exert more control when things around you feel out of control.

A few years ago I attended a lecture by leadership expert Dr Anthony Kasozi[45]. He offered the following insight into how we respond to the VUCA world around us:

'Faced with complexity and ambiguity – we naturally seek control. We want to make sure that what happens next is more expected, and its impact on us less unpredictable...'

So what do you actually have control over in this world? Take a moment to think about all the things in your life and work that you feel you can control.

In reality, there is only one thing that you actually have control over and that's yourself and your reaction to things. And as we've seen when we looked at triggers, even controlling our own reactions to things can be hard. I'd like you to really connect with this principle.

You have no actual control over anything in this world other than your own behaviour and reactions.

You can choose to try and influence things, but you can't actually control their outcome. I offer this as a lens to look through when you are stuck with something and feeling

---

45 http://anthonykasozi.info/

frustrated. You have a choice of where to expend your energy: you can focus on trying to control, or you can focus on your own behaviour and trying to influence where you can.

In this context, control is trying to get to your own goal while looking through your own ladder of inference. Needing to control is strongly associated with not being open, while influencing is taking a real interest in the other person's ladder of inference and viewpoint and having conversations to see if they can find their own way towards your goal. Influence is strongly associated with the capacity to be open.

When facing a challenge, the model below will help you look at the frustrations you are facing and decide where to put your energy – into managing your own behaviour or into influencing people.

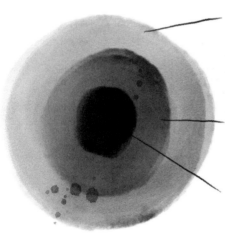

Can't control, influence or change
(What things are out of your control? What can you do to reduce your focus on these things?)

Can influence & change – but you can't control
(What things can you influence and change? How might you go about doing that?)

Can control...
your behaviour & your thoughts
(What things are you likely to have to respond to? How would you like to respond to them in an ideal world?)

Circles of influence and control

Restoring your resilience

This may not be an exercise you need right now. It's here for you to reference at a point when you are feeling overwhelmed with too much going on. The purpose of this exercise is to help you take action and make some choices that will restore your resilience.

1   In relation to the thing you are stuck on, write a brain dump of all the things that you are feeling and what is frustrating you? Don't filter it or judge anything before you write – just get it all out.

2   Think about the things that are frustrating you and plot them on the control model on your worksheet.

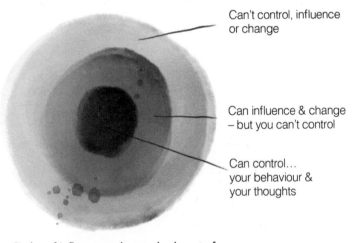

Can't control, influence or change

Can influence & change – but you can't control

Can control... your behaviour & your thoughts

Circles of influence and control: where to focus

What are the things that you have control over (the centre circle)? For example, checking your emails when you don't want to. You have control over whether or not you do that. Make a list of actions you can take to reduce your frustrations. Get yourself unstuck. If your little voice is saying you can't take the actions you feel you want to, use the perspective check from earlier on page 142.

Accept that you have no control over the things in the second circle. Use your energy to think about who you need to influence and what requests you could make so your ideal outcome is more likely. Again, if your little voice is saying you can't make a request you feel you want to, use the perspective check.

For things you can't even influence (the outside circle), work to reduce your focus on these. Use your energy to focus on the centre and middle circles.

REFLECTION

This chapter on taking care of yourself builds on Chapter 2 Helpers and hinderers and focuses on getting yourself back into action towards your most nourished self. Take some time to pull together what you now know from this chapter.

> *What I now know about how to move myself into action when I'm stuck:*

> *What I now know about my energy and how to use it:*

> *What I now know about my resilience and how to manage it:*

> *What the above knowledge means to me:*

CHAPTER 6

Emergence

INTRODUCTION

As you've worked through this book you've grown your self-awareness, had some insights that have demanded action and developed your understanding of what choices will nourish your success. These final two chapters, Emergence and Sustain, are where you pull together all of your thinking into a set of thoughts, actions and reflections. They combine to give you your road map to move forward from this point.

The Cambridge English Dictionary defines emergence as 'the fact of something becoming known or starting to exist'. The emerging knowledge you have about yourself will give rise to an altered version of who you are and how you behave. You're obviously still the same person, but your response and reaction to certain situations will have changed and your views on any number of things will have a different perspective. Overall, the relationship with your drive will be starting to shift. It won't be shifting in a way that diminishes what you can achieve; rather, it will be shifting in a way that allows you to sustain your success for longer. In my coaching work, my purpose is to help clients arrive at the insights that will move them forward, to give them tools and techniques to be self-sufficient and no longer need my support. This is the intention in this book also.

When clients reflect on what they now know about themselves they frequently describe their emergence by looking at their reactions to specific events. For example, 'When x happens I now do y. This is so different. The old me would have…' When they speak there is often a sense of wonder at how different the old version of them was and a strong feeling that they can't imagine stepping back into some of their old ways of thinking and behaviours. This language of the 'old me' versus the 'new me' is something that people who have gone through some kind of personal transformation often use.

After my breakdown and the subsequent work that I did on my relationship with my drive, I returned to work feeling very different, in a good way. I was still able to perform really well, but I noticed that the quality of my relationships had improved. I felt like I was fighting less. My ability to see the other person's point of view and move away from my attachment to being right had shifted massively. So much so, that one colleague who I had worked with for over eight years commented on how much he was enjoying working with me. This was extraordinary as we had previously had a pretty adversarial relationship. He was really generous in his acknowledgements and asked me how I'd managed to change so much. The old me would have heard this as patronising and would probably have been triggered by him daring to comment on my behaviour. The new me was able to accept his words for what they were – genuine recognition of a positive shift. I remain friends with that colleague, and he has been through his own transformation over time. We now laugh together at the 'old versions' of us.

TIPS ON HOW TO REFLECT

This chapter is all about reflection and will help you tune into the emerging version of you. Here are a few hints and tips on how to deepen your reflection over and above what you've done to this point.

Take your reflection beyond the first level

When you are reflecting, an initial answer will come to you. Going beyond that first level reflection is powerful as it will help you see how useful the reflection is and how deep it might run. To get beyond that first level, it's important to ask yourself some additional questions. I call these 'reflection-build questions' as they enhance your self-awareness and understanding.

These are examples of the types of questions I asked myself regarding one of my insights:

Reflection question: Now you know you have a tendency to think rather than feel, what strategies will you use to help you make big decisions?

Answer: I will notice the fast (thinking) decision I make, but maybe sit with that for a time while I try to connect with how I feel about that decision.

Reflection-build question: If you can connect with how you feel about a decision, what will that allow you to do?

Answer: It will stop me taking on more than I need to (if I don't really want to) and, actually, now I think of it, the pause will stop me offering to help everyone all the time! It might stop that offer coming out of my mouth before I've noticed it was there.

Over time and with more practice you can go deeper than this. Unconscious patterns and learned behaviours don't change overnight, but the good news is that neuroscientists now know that the brain has the ability to reorganise itself by forming new neural connections throughout life. They call this neuro-plasticity. By reflecting and bringing your awareness to your ingrained behaviours, it is absolutely possible to rewire the brain. The 'but that's just how I am excuse' is no longer valid. If you want to change, you can.

Beware of a binary mindset

While useful to some extent, the 'old me' and 'new me' ideology also represents a very binary mindset. It's black and white – either/or. A useful way to reflect is to allow your thoughts to work with the concept of 'part of you'. Here's an example of how that would work:

> *Reflection question: If someone triggers you with one of your biggest triggers, how would you now react?*
>
> *Answer: Part of me would like to do x, but another part of me would like to do y. Knowing what I now know, I would choose to do y.*
>
> *Reflection-build question: If you choose to do y, how does that make things better?*
>
> *Answer: By doing y,... (benefits listed).*

Really connecting with the benefits of your new behaviour will help prevent you slipping back into your previous ways – things you have identified you want to change.

Theresa, an Operations Director, had been working on her relationship with one of her direct reports who she found very frustrating. The direct report was a person who loved lots of detail and would ask lots of questions around any request. Theresa would initially find the questioning OK, but would soon get really triggered and think, 'Oh, for goodness' sake, stop asking questions and just get on with it'. The trigger would leak out in the tone of her conversation with her colleague.

Over time, this pattern played out again and again. Theresa had got to the point where she would be very directive with her colleague in an attempt to try and avoid the barrage of questions. During our work together, her self-awareness grew. Theresa recognised that she wasn't valuing the difference in viewpoint her colleague brought. Her insight was that by becoming more directive and prescriptive she was inadvertently taking responsibility for how her colleague did things. When things went wrong her colleague's response was, 'Well you told me to do that'. Here's how Theresa reflected in our coaching conversation:

My reflection question: How do you brief your colleague now, and how do you respond to her need to ask questions?

Theresa's answer: I brief her by explaining the context of what my request is (the why) and then explain what I think the output needs to look like. I then ask her to take some time (length of time depends on what the request is) to consider the request and come back to me with questions. I also ask for suggestions on whether the output needs to be any different. Part of me still dreads and gets frustrated by the follow-up meeting where she asks me questions, but the other part of me knows that her questions are coming from a good place.

My reflection-build question: By you changing your approach what is that making possible?

Answer: Well, she is much more motivated and comes up with some great ideas (as well as still asking questions). Now, when things go wrong, we have a good discussion about how to move forward – a discussion that she is engaged in. She is taking responsibility for her work and not blaming mistakes on how I briefed her. We even go and have coffee together and chat now.

So, as you think about the version of you that is emerging, ask yourself those reflection-build questions and be aware if your thinking becomes too binary.

Patterns and beliefs

When you are reflecting your brain will naturally relate back to your ladder of inference, pulling through your past experience to help you make sense of the world. As you reflect in this chapter, continue to pay attention to the beliefs and/or patterns that are present in your thinking. Draw on your skills of being open to bring challenge to those beliefs and opinions.

The two exercises that follow have no online worksheet because I don't want to restrict how you capture your reflections. Think back to your preferred way of capturing your thoughts that you used in Chapter 4 Insight; you may find that approach useful again here.

John, a finance director, had a foundational belief that his view of how to do things was right. He was highly qualified, highly experienced and had a hugely strong track record. His company had a well-renowned graduate entry scheme and he would have graduates moving through his team on rotation, for a period of six months each time. He got on well with graduates for whom finance wasn't their core area of skill/interest, but really struggled to get on with graduates who wanted to end up with a role in finance. The company was investing a lot in the graduate programme and John was the only director who wasn't keeping graduates in his team at the end of their programme – they all chose to leave.

After working together over a period of six months, John had a significant insight that allowed him to let go of his core belief that his view of the world was the right one – a huge shift for him and one that improved his relationships with the finance-focused graduates. His new belief meant he was able to listen to other views that were brought to him, he was able to properly hear what was being said as his inner voice wasn't shouting, 'What do you know?' His shift led to him retaining a great calibre person within eight months, and to him learning from the graduates. To help him reflect I replayed to him one of his comments from our first coaching session: 'You can't teach an old dog new tricks.' He laughed. 'Did I say that? Well, here I am now and who knew there were tricks this old dog didn't even know about!'

Emerging shifts in mindset and beliefs

This exercise will help you get to know the version of you that is emerging. I have a series of questions to help you, but let your thinking go wherever it needs to and take your time (maybe a few days) to complete this.

CATALYSTS (CHAPTER 1)

1   What am I now noticing about the catalysts I wanted to pay attention to?

HELPERS AND HINDERERS (CHAPTER 2)

2   What has changed in how I am using my helpers and hinderers?
3   What else would I like to change?

OPENNESS (CHAPTER 3)

4   How has my capacity to be open shifted?
5   What are other people seeing in me?

INSIGHT (CHAPTER 4)

6   Which insights have had the most powerful impact on me?
7   What actions have/will come about as a result of these insights?

CARE (CHAPTER 5)

8   What strategies am I now using to maintain my resilience and help me get unstuck?

EMERGENCE (CHAPTER 6)

9   The beliefs and values I am taking forward with me as strongly as before about:

   a)   myself are...

   b)   my colleagues are...

   c)   my family and friends are...

   d)   the world around me are...

10   How do these beliefs nourish my success in a sustainable way?

11   The beliefs and values that have softened or changed about:

   a)   myself are...

   b)   my colleagues are...

   c)   my family and friends are...

   d)   the world around me is...

12   How does the softening of beliefs nourish my success in a sustainable way?

THE STORY OF THE EMERGING YOU

Storytelling is an age-old method of communication that's known to have many benefits. There is a plethora of storytelling theories, frameworks and applications. Stories are part of our everyday life. Every time we talk to a colleague about something we are telling a story. If you talk to a number of different colleagues about the same story, the story will evolve. You may find you embellish parts of the story depending on the audience – this is something we do naturally. We use storytelling as a way of connecting with people.

We know our brains have neuroplasticity so we can train them to change narrative if we want to. Thus, we can change our own feelings about past events by telling ourselves a different version of the story. I'm not talking about creating stories that are fiction; that would create a world of fantasists. I'm talking about shifting the emphasis and focusing on different parts of what happened; looking for the characters, the events, the nuances that help us engage with the world in the way that is most useful for us.

People who have the ability to think positively in the face of adversity demonstrate this well. My mum is a great example of this. When my father was having chemotherapy and his hair was falling out, this was the story mum told me on the phone: 'Dad had another round of chemo today and his hair is coming out quickly now. It's good it's happening in spring as we can put his hair out in the garden for the birds to come and take for their nests.' So their story was about spring and birds and the optimism around that, rather than the horror of terminal cancer and treatment. And in the telling of that story, my questions that followed her story were about the type of birds that were taking the hair, rather than asking how dad was at the hospital. We did have those darker conversations, but the different narratives and stories were hugely helpful in helping us through a challenging time.

Telling the story of the emerging you

Create some time and the environment to get creative. You choose how to tell your story: handwrite, type, record, draw. Whatever method you choose have fun with it, *feel* what comes up as you tell the story of the emerging you. It's important that you have a 'fixed' record of the story in some way. Something you can re-read or re-listen to.

STORY 1

This story starts today. Write (or talk) about the qualities, values and beliefs of the person you are right now. Explore what these make possible for you and your success (whatever elements of your life combine to make your definition of success). Describe what success feels like when it's nourishing, as well as what it feels like when success is coming at too much of a cost. Include other characters in your story: those who will keep you moving forward and growing; and those whose companionship, energy and counsel you value or who value yours. Think about some protagonists or events that bring challenge and how your new self would respond to that.

Leave some time (maybe a week or so) before you come to the next story. During that week re-read/re-listen to your first story a few times.

STORY 2

The leading character in this next story is the version of you who started reading this book. How would your first story be different when told by the 'old' you?

- How do you feel about this second story when compared with the first story?
- Which story will you choose as your narrative to take forward?

This is an exercise you may want to repeat, play with and explore over time.

REFLECTION

Take some time now to reflect on what you know about your emerging self.

> *How strong is your connection with your emerging self?*

> *Looking at your emerging shifts in mindset and beliefs, in which areas do you have the sense of most difference compared with your thinking at the start of this book?*

> How could you build reflection into your life as a regular practice?

> *To what extent has your first, new, story motivated you to sustain the version of you that will nourish your success from this point forward?*

CHAPTER 7

INTRODUCTION

Through this programme you will have got to know yourself better. Some of what you've learned may have surprised you; some you might not have liked. But all this knowledge is now with you to make choices on how you move forward. You understand and are connected with the emerging you. This final chapter will give you the tools and techniques to sustain that version of you; the one who allows you to nourish and sustain your success.

The exercises in this chapter are presented in two sections:

- Setting your foundations and boundaries for success: three exercises for you to do now.
- Nourishing success checkpoints – four exercises for you to come back to at intervals of your choosing or when you get stuck.

SETTING YOUR FOUNDATIONS AND BOUNDARIES FOR SUCCESS

The following three exercises will ground you in the key things that you need to pay attention to in order to sustain the version of you that has emerged through this programme.

Non-negotiables

You will now feel like you really understand the things that energise you and build your resilience (mind, body and spirit), but what foundational things, if lost from your daily/ weekly/monthly routine, would have a negative effect on you very quickly? What losses could put holes or dents in your resilience bucket or trigger some of those unwanted responses?

I encourage you to think of these foundational things as non-negotiable in how you move through your life from this point forward. I've seen these things range from taking a 30-minute walk at lunchtime (or at some point during the day) to needing to speak to a child before bedtime (and making that work wherever in the world my client is). Remember, these are your needs and it's OK for you to protect them in your schedule. If you let go of your non-negotiables, you are choosing to hurt yourself (even if it's just in the short term). Letting go of your non-negotiables is the very opposite of nourishing your success. You could think of this as your celebrity rider to success. If bathing in milk once a week is your thing, go for it! Make a list on the worksheet or somewhere you can easily refer back to.

Description of my non-negotiable	Frequency of it needing to happen

If your non-negotiables are things that fall into your work day, add them to your diary (you can of course mark it as private time if you need to). Tell people who can access your diary that the time blocked out is important to you and agree/request they don't book meetings over it.

There may, of course, be times where they slip, but your focus is to commit. You're driven, so even things that you know are your non-negotiables will sometimes slip more often than you would like. If you feel this happening, ask yourself the following:

1   How often has the non-negotiable slipped?

2   Is there one particular non-negotiable that I 'give away' more often than others?

3   What is it about this non-negotiable that causes me to readily give it up? What does my inner voice say about it?

4   What was it that took priority?

5   Why, in that moment, did I see my non-negotiable as less important?

6   On reflection, did I make a good choice to let my non-negotiable go?

7   Are there any patterns in my thinking around letting my non-negotiables slip?

If you are regularly letting one non-negotiable slip, consider making choices on how you protect the non-negotiable *or* recalibrate – is it still a non-negotiable?

Recalibration is fine, and actually very important. Think back to the work you did on identifying your energy patterns. You may find your non-negotiables shift as the seasons change. If you have identified this, add your notes under frequency in the table above.

Traffic light warnings

As a result of the work you've done so far, you will be getting better at tuning into the optimum choices you need to make. However, you are human, so it's important to have a method that helps prevent you from slipping back into old habits (i.e. making choices that are not going to nourish you). RAG (red, amber, green) traffic light reporting is a common reporting framework in the corporate world, but you can also use it personally to stay on track with your choices.

This exercise relates the RAG warning back to the stress curve you saw in Chapter 2 on page 29.

- Green is when everything is going well; you are operating at your most energised and your stress levels are in that optimum place. You are performing at your highest capacity.
- Amber is when you are moving backwards and forwards between eustress and distress, and the short-term choices you are making are creating further stress on you. (You looked at these in Chapter 2 Helpers and hinderers.)
- Red is when you are in the distress zone and you have lost sight of how the choices you are making are contributing further to your stress. Your drive is pushing

you forward. You are not able to see things for what they are. You are continuing to make short-term choices that are hindering your success.

Stress curve (source: Yerkes–Dodson law 1908)

Have your worksheet beside you as you read on.

1   Look back to your wheel of focus exercise (Chapter 1, page 19) and the elements you identified as being most important to you. Given what you now know about yourself, which are the areas where you are less likely to make nourishing choices? Note the areas on the first column in the worksheet table.

2   Looking at your list, for each area complete:

   a)   column 2: what is the first type of behaviour or thinking that might suggest you are not making nourishing choices? These are your amber warnings.

   b)   column 3: what are the signs that things have shifted to being a red warning?

Here's an extract from my traffic light warnings as an example:

	Amber	Red light warning
Exercise	Getting cross about not being able to make exercise classes. Starting to get into black and white thinking and not fitting in even a 20-minute walk or yoga session as 'not worth it'.	Doing lots of high-energy exercise, getting up early/ doing exercise late to fit it in *or* dropping exercise altogether (as only high energy is enough).
Family (first level)	Not looking at family WhatsApp for a few days.	Not calling mum for over two weeks.
Friends	Cancelling social arrangements at short notice.	Not even accepting social arrangements and getting defensive when challenged.
Nutrition	Starting to drop green vegetables and opting for starchy foods. Red wine during the week.	Drinking more than two cups of coffee a day. Eating late. More than two bottles of wine over a week. Starchy foods shifting into chocolate.

	Amber	Red light warning
Sleep	Less than eight hours a night for more than three days.	Less than seven hours sleep and/or less than eight hours for more than five days.
Social media	Waking up and looking at Instagram and Twitter first thing, then at regular intervals during the day.	More frequent checking, including when watching television at night.

This grid will help you notice what's happening. You can then refer back to your helpers and make choices that will nourish you and help you get back into the high-performing eustress zone.

CATALYST CONVERTORS

To help you gain perspective on your own behaviour and drive, I have encouraged you to consult people during a number of the exercises you have completed. It is normal for people to help you see things we can't. No matter how much work you do on your self-awareness, the views of others will always give you another perspective that can be useful, and potentially lead to new insights. Luft and Ingham's Johari window model[46]

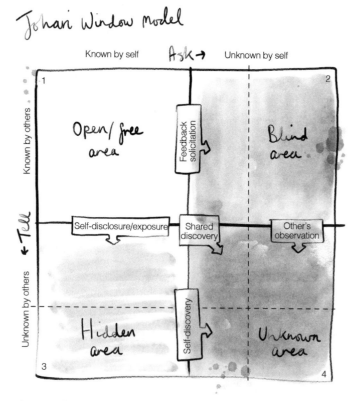

Johari window model

46 Luft, J. and Ingham, H. (1955) 'The Johari window, a graphic model of interpersonal awareness', Proceedings of the western training laboratory in group development, University of California, Los Angeles

is a useful visual way of illustrating this and reminds us that we don't know everything about ourselves.

Throughout this book you will have stretched your self-understanding not only into area 3 on this model, you'll also have made choices on what you choose to share and what is for only you to know. You'll also have stretched your awareness into area 2, which would not have been possible without the input of others.

Choosing catalyst convertors

You now have the option to specially ask people to help you sustain your success – I call these people your catalyst convertors. Think back to the people who worked with you during the exercises. Who were the most insightful collaborators (even if what they offered was hard to hear in the first instance)? I strongly recommend you talk to these people about what you've already achieved, and your intention to sustain the version of you that has emerged from this process. Request them to be part of your future journey by being a catalyst convertor with you. Share your traffic light warning exercise with them; they may even have things to add!

Most importantly, agree with them how you want them to call you out. How do you want them to challenge you when they observe you going beyond the edges of what you have decided are your new boundaries; those amber and red behaviours? Pay particular attention to how you want them to flag a red-light warning. In my experience, once you are so absorbed with work that you are in a red-light warning situation, anyone trying to call you out could feel like they are coming into a lion's den. Think about your triggers; when your drive goes into overdrive it can be very intimidating. Think creatively about how you would hear them in the midst of that absorption in your drive.

> *I had one client who gave his catalyst convertors red cards to use with him. They all agreed that they could give him as many red cards as they felt he needed before he took notice. (It took four red cards over one month on one occasion.)*

NOURISHING SUCCESS CHECKPOINTS

These are exercises for you to come back to when you find yourself being drawn back to old unwanted habits. The use of the word 'when' is deliberate. You are human, and your system 1 thinking (fast) will take a while to be reprogrammed with the mindset and behaviour shifts you want to make.

Body check

Look back at your notes on the physiological catalyst identifier exercise (Chapter 1, page 10) and combine this with what you now know about your helpers and hinderers. Consider the experiences you've had putting different things into action over the course of your work with this methodology.

1   On the worksheet, mark on the body map below the symptoms that you believe are linked to you slipping into the distress zone on the stress curve.

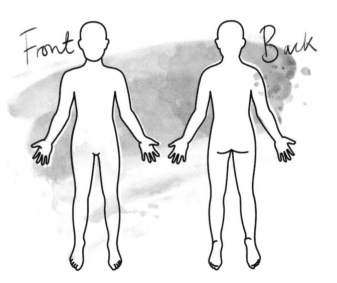

2 Looking at the above and carrying on the traffic light warning approach, grab an amber/orange and red pen. Identify the symptoms that demand greatest attention (i.e. they suggest you've slipped into the red alert zone) and those you need to pay some heed to (amber zone). Circle them with the appropriate colour.

The next time you notice unusual or unwanted physiological symptoms, come back to this. I can guarantee that you will forget the link between some physical symptoms and stress. When we are driven, success and the buzz from being busy release those lovely hormones adrenaline and cortisol that we discussed when looking at helpers and hinderers. The feeling of power those hormones give us reduces our capacity to tune into what's actually going on for us.

I had a very powerful reminder of this in the process of writing this book. You may remember reading that I used to regularly suffer from excruciating pain under the left-hand side of my ribcage while in meetings. I used to have to move around in my seat, get up and walk around. I was tested for all sorts of things and nothing was found. I'd forgotten about that pain, as it disappeared after I started paying attention to how I was nourishing my success. Then, in the course of writing this book, I spent one full day writing the hardest part of my story. That evening, the exact same pain under my rib returned and I started thinking, 'What have I eaten today, have I done any core exercises that could have caused it?' Then I realised my body had been triggered into stress by bringing up some very painful memories, and this feeling was just part of that. It passed and hasn't come back since. Our bodies and minds are truly extraordinary.

Habit check

As part of your work looking at your helpers and hinderers, there will be some deeply ingrained habits and thoughts that you have decided to change.

Anything that is deeply ingrained is hard to shift. Be ready to have an ongoing love/hate relationship with some of these old habits and thoughts. Especially those that you used to believe served you well, but that you now have a different perspective on.

Combine your thinking from Chapter 6 Emergence with the understanding of your triggers and resilience factors. Use this understanding to complete the worksheet grid. This gives you a focused version of the areas of shift for you. Keep this to no more than seven habits or thoughts – the ones that have the greatest impact on the nourishment of your success.

Previous habit/ thought	Preferred habit/ thought	Level of challenge in keeping the preferred habit/ thought going (high, medium or low)	Triggers that could pull me back to the old habit/ thought

This checklist is something to come back to after you or your catalyst converters have raised an amber or red flag. When that happens, look at your list and think about what has happened in the run up to noticing the amber/red flag. Which habits and thoughts have slipped back in?

Over time, you'll get to know which habits can slip back in for a while with no detrimental effect, and which ones have the potential to have a more negative effect on your success.

Success first-aid kit

Imagine the scenario where you or your catalyst converters have noticed an amber or red warning. It's useful to have identified your go-to, first level renew/recharge choices. With the new insights and knowledge that you've gained, choose the things that can have the most impact in nourishing you, making sure you include a mixture of things that cover mind, body and spirit. That might sound a little grand but, if you only focus on one dimension, the other elements may remain off kilter. This is a simple exercise but, again, our brains in overdrive can make us forget the things that we need.

Write notes around the empty first-aid kit listing the things you would pack in here.

Relationship with success check

This book is all about making choices that nourish your success. You love your work so it's a key part of your life and your identity. However, having worked through the programme, now is the time to reflect on whether anything has shifted in how you measure your success.

1   Imagine a life where all the important things you have identified throughout this book are in place and your work is going really well.

●   In relation to success, how does this scenario feel?

2   Now imagine a life where the important things you have identified throughout this book are in place *but* your work is not going so well.

●   In relation to success, how does this scenario feel?

As you consider your response to question 2, notice your inner voice. Which of the following two voices are you hearing?

●   Supporter: cheering you on and celebrating that you made the decisions that were right for your all-round wellbeing and success. Acknowledging and valuing that even when you make nourishing choices, your drive probably means you will deliver more than someone who is less driven.

or

●   Adversary: criticising you for making those nourishing choices, berating you (even a little bit) with a narrative like: 'You should have worked that weekend. If you hadn't gone to the x, y and z thing you'd committed to, you could have been more successful.'

If you are hearing your supporter, you have shifted to a relationship with your drive and success that is more sustainable for all the areas in your life you have identified. Great news!

If you are hearing your adversary, you'll find it much harder to nourish your success and sustain it in the long term. There is a higher potential you'll be pulled back into a damaging spiral of work success dominating all other forms of success. It might be time to find an executive coach to help you.

NEED SOME EXTRA SUPPORT TO MOVE YOU FORWARD?

You have covered a significant amount of ground in working through this book. Yet, even with the help of friends, families and colleagues, actually doing the things you know you want to can be challenging, especially when that in-built drive is pushing you forward. Sometimes you need to dip into specific things that keep coming up (and holding you back) to really find out what's going on for you – so you can move forward. And that can be hard to do without professional input.

How to choose an executive coach

Enlisting the support of a coach to help you move forward is a great investment. The field of executive coaching is growing and growing, and there are thousands of practitioners out there.

When looking for a coach, here are my recommendations:

- Word of mouth: ask around to see if any of your colleagues have someone they can recommend.

- Choose someone who has a recognised coaching qualification and/or an accreditation with a professional body such as the AC (Association for Coaching), the EMCC (European Coaching and Mentoring Council), ICF (International Coach Federation) or APECS (Association for Professional Executive Coaching and Supervision). Without this, you may be working with someone who does not fully understand the ethics and morals involved in coaching.

- Insist on a no-charge chemistry session with your potential coach lasting at least 45 minutes. The relationship with a coach is very personal. You will say things to that person that you may never say out loud to anyone else. It is imperative that you feel you have a rapport with your coach and respect and trust them.

- Commit to a minimum of three sessions (each between 60 and 90 minutes). You need the discipline of working with your coach over at least three sessions to set yourself actions and see how things move forward.

- A good executive coach doesn't need any experience in the field you come from. The skill of a coach is in choosing great questions to allow you to arrive at insights that move you forward. However, my personal view is that an executive coach who has senior level business experience brings a level of understanding and empathy with the many challenges faced in leadership. This experience helps the coach find the most powerful questions to ask you to push you forward to achieve your goals.

Coaching or counselling?

Some readers may find that deep emotions surface while reading this book. Some who have followed this programme in the past have asked me whether coaching is right for them, or whether counselling would be more appropriate. Given their questions, I thought it worth including some guidance on this.

Both coaching and counselling have the goal of helping you move forward in a way that you feel happy about. The terms are often used interchangeably, and this ambiguity is for good reason. We are complicated beings and, as such, our whole selves (past and present) impact how we are now and what our future might look like. It is useful to think of coaching and counselling on a spectrum, where each discipline will move to and fro along the spectrum during conversations. To help you decide whether coaching or counselling is your starting point, look at the grid below. Do you feel more drawn to the focus on the left (coaching) or on the right (counselling)?

Coaching		Counselling
←		→
Action orientated		Coping orientated
Helps you recognise what you think		Helps you understand how you feel
Helps you set and achieve goals		Helps you recognise and solve problems
Challenge		Empathy
Present and future focus		Focus on the past
Focus on potential		Focus on being at peace with yourself
Trained to helping you move forward		Trained to deal with mental health conditions (e.g. anxiety, addiction, defined disorders)

As a coaching practitioner, I move across the spectrum depending on the needs of my client, but my broad focus is on the left. I will move to the right when it is appropriate and beneficial to help a client move forward. However, for some clients, we find that we are spending a lot of time being drawn to the past and that there is something there that needs exploring before there is the capability and freedom to move forward. In those instances, I would make this observation and discuss with my client. On every occasion this has happened, my clients have valued the observation, chosen to have some counselling and have then come back to coaching when they have greater capacity for being future focused.

Whatever support you choose, you are making a positive choice to improve your life.

YOUR NEXT CHAPTER

It's been a privilege to share my experiences and knowledge with you. In working through my own relationship with my drive, I remember wanting a 'manual' to help me understand how to move forward. There wasn't one place I could go to for all the information I needed; much of the literature was in the territory of work-life balance, which wasn't what I was looking for. There was nothing that spoke to my drive to succeed. So, over the last 20 years, I've been consuming and devouring a massive range of information and experiences that have combined into this programme.

My hope is that this book, with its well-thumbed pages and your notes, feels like a companion; a guide who is now with you as you move into the next chapter of your life; a friend who can help remind you of what you once knew about yourself, and help you use that knowledge to your benefit; someone who is there to refer back to when needed.

I wish for you a life that is successful and nourished in all the areas you want it to be.

ACKNOWLEDGEMENTS

Thank you, Sue Richardson. I listened to you speak about the 'seven P's of publishing for business books' in October 2017. You threw a question out to the audience: 'Who has a book in them?' A surprising number of people raised their hands. You then started talking about Purpose being one of the most important things to have clear if you are considering being an author. In that moment I had an epiphany. I could help more people in their careers if I wrote a book – I'd reach a wider audience. During the two weeks after that epiphany my brain was wired – it sliced and diced all my experiences to date and the framework for the Choices™ programme was born. As my independent publisher, you and your brilliant team have supported me through the writing, editing, design and publication of this book. As my book coach, you have helped me become a writer. You are now a great friend, red wine and cinema buddy.

Thank you to my clients and colleagues – some of your stories appear here (anonymised). You inspired me to see that there was a need for this book.

Thank you, Amanda, Ian and Beth. You were my test-readers. Giving my draft manuscript to you was like handing over a newborn, but I knew it was in great hands. Your comments on the draft were invaluable, and made this finished product all the more powerful.

Thank you also to my final manuscript readers. Your generous testimonials reinforced my belief that this book will help people (and I'm delighted that it helped each of you!).

Thank you, Rebecca Jones. I first met you on the Kaliyoga retreat in Spain in 2017, where your nutrition advice gave me the information I'd been missing. Our follow-up one-to-one work further supported me to make changes that are now completely embedded in my life. Thank you for lending me your expert brain to help form the nutrition references in Chapter 2.

Thank you, early readers. You generously gave your time and testimonials. Your insights will help potential readers find this book.

Thank you, Sue White. As my coach/supervisor, your wisdom, experience, challenge and encouragement will continue to help me be the best coach I can be.

Thank you, Kate Stillman. We worked together for over two years after my breakdown, and continue to work together on an ad hoc basis. Your support and expertise contributed to the emergence of who I am now.

Thank you to my family for always supporting what I choose to do – even if there is a loving eye-roll of 'Here she goes again' now and then!

Thank you to my girlfriends (and respective partners) of many and recent years. You all help me in different ways. I love you all: Mandy and Ricardo; Sarah and Adam; Tansie and Steve; Linda and Simon; Paul and Yvonne; Jackie and Nick; Caroline; Mandy S; Luke and Saffron; SJ and Jim; Martin and Maria; Ingrid; Hazel and Sal. I am giggling now because I know Linda will want to know why she wasn't first on the list! Linda – I've listed you all in order of how long I've known you!

Thank you, Laurie Holdsworth. You helped give me the confidence to weave my own story through this book. Many adults weren't so sure but, as a wise 16-year-old, you were unequivocal in your belief that my story would add credibility.

Thank you, Phil Holdsworth. As my partner, you've been alongside me through some of the most difficult times of my life (while you were going through your own stuff). You ground me, give me unquestioning support, but also space to be me. And you never ever judge. I love you.

And, finally, these acknowledgements wouldn't be complete without an in-memoriam thank you to my ex-husband. Thank you, Simon. We were married for 14 years. We had many good years, but you never found a way to live with your bipolar disorder and life experience. I know your demons are silenced now and you are at peace.